RAINCOAST CHRONICLES 12

Edited by
Howard White

HARBOUR PUBLISHING

RAINCOAST CHRONICLES 12
Copyright© 1990 by Harbour Publishing

Published by Harbour Publishing, Box 219, Madeira Park, BC, Canada V0N 2H0

Editorial Assistant: Alec Macaulay
Design: Gaye Hammond
Cover design: Roger Handling
Photographs and Illustrations:
    Front and back covers courtesy Alan Haig-Brown; 1, 2, 3, 5, 7, courtesy A.J. Spilsbury; 8, photo by Jim Ryan; 9, 11, 14, 15, 16, 17, 18, 19, 20, Macmillan Bloedel Audio Visual Services Corporate Advertising; 12, A.M. Feast; 21, Ministry of Forests #22798/2; 23, 24, 25, 27, 29, courtesy Edith Iglauer; 30, 31, 39, 42, courtesy Mrs. D.W. Steele; 32, 33, 34, 35, 36, 37, courtesy Lillian Lamont-Bateman; 43, 48, courtesy Elphinstone Pioneer Museum, Gibsons; 45, 50, courtesy John Watson; 46, courtesy Vancouver Maritime Museum; 49, Harbour Publishing; 52, 55 (bottom), 57, 59 photo by Alan Haig-Brown; 53, John Mailer/ Public Archives of Canada/ PA 145355; 54, John Mailer/ Public Archives of Canada/ PA 145357; 55, (top) Finning Tractor photo; 56, (top) John Mailer/ Public Archives of Canada/ PA 145361; 56, (bottom) Public Archives of Canada/PA 146255; 58, photo courtesy Alan Haig-Brown; 64, 65, 66, 68, 70, 71, 72, 75, 76, courtesy Gordon Ballentine.
    Illustrations on pages 60 and 63 by Maurice Spira.
    Illustration on page 29 by Bus Griffiths
    Maps on page 40 by John Watson

Printed and bound in Canada

CANADIAN CATALOGUING IN PUBLICATION DATA

Main entry under title:

Raincoast chronicles 12

    ISBN 1-55017-028-7

    1. Pacific Coast (B.C.) — History.   2. Pacific Coast (B.C.) — Social
life and customs.   I. White, Howard, 1945–
FC3803.R34 1990   971.1   C90-091600-1
F1087.5.R34 1990

CONTENTS

INTRODUCTION

Amazingly, it is now eighteen years since Howard White penned his first *Raincoast Chronicles* editorial boldly declaring his intention to create a quarterly journal that would place BC coast *character* on the record, and furthermore, to produce said journal *quarterly*.

With twelve issues in eighteen years we have fallen a mite short in the frequency department—but we have the excuse that the journal evolved into a serial book, then into a full-blown book publishing operation that has now put out well over a hundred individual titles dealing with all facets of life on the coast.

Our success in the character-recording department is harder to measure but we did receive a hopeful sign last summer when editor White was summoned to appear before the annual general meeting of the Canadian Historical Association at Laval University in Quebec City to receive a CHA Career Award "for Raincoast Chronicles and the Promotion of Regional History." The citation read by Professor Paul La Roque of the University of Quebec stated, "For the past several decades Howard White has been a tireless promoter and creator of quality British Columbia regional history. Through his imaginative *Raincoast Chronicles* and Harbour Publishing he has nurtured and brought into being a remarkable range of work which captures the essence of British Columbia, particularly the coastal region. White has markedly enhanced our knowledge and understanding."

We've received other awards over the years, but there's something about this one that gave all of us connected with the Raincoast project a specially warm glow.

We're happy to welcome back two of our most popular contributors this issue—**Jim Spilsbury** and **Edith Iglauer**. Jim, the aviation and radio pioneer who co-wrote the bestsellers *Spilsbury's Coast* and *The Accidental Airline*, treats us to a hilarious account of early logging on Savary Island. Edith returns to the subject of her bestselling book, *Fishing With John*, to recount a fishboat excursion she made with her late husband **John Daly** to Bella Coola.

Other highlights include "The Gentle Giants of Sproat Lake" by **A.M. Feast**, an account of the famous **Martin Mars** waterbombers; a loving testament to the classic wooden seiner *Chief Y* by **Alan Haig-Brown**; a breathtaking account by **Howard White** of a world-record-setting dash for the Langdale ferry in a '73 Volvo; an account of barnacled bush flying by pioneer aviator **Gordon Ballentine**; and captivating memoirs of early Stillwater by **Lillian Lamont Bateman**, and of early Gibsons by **John Watson**.

LOGGING
on
SAVARY ISLAND

A.J. Spilsbury

OF ALL THE PLACES my parents could have chosen to scratch out a living, Savary Island had to be one of the worst choices. There were only a half dozen families living year-round there at the best of times. It is extremely beautiful with its magnificent beach but there is no easy access, no running water, and there has never been any local industry to provide jobs, then or now. From time to time though, the hand-to-mouth existence of the Savary Island "permanents" would be brightened for a brief period by paid work in logging, when some reckless soul would decide to have another go at the island's hard-luck timber.

I'm going to take a wild guess and say that Louis Anderson built his first house on Savary around about 1900 or 1905. This was ten years or so after Jack Green, the original resident, had been murdered. Anyway, Louis Anderson had a much younger brother-in-law, W.C. (Bill) Palmer, the youngest member of the large, well-known Palmer family of loggers that came up from Oregon in the last century and staked a farm at the head of Theodosia Arm where the old folks lived and died and the boys all became loggers. Bill Palmer at that time owned one of the very first steam donkey engines. It had only one drum, which was not really a drum but a vertical spool or capstan. The cable was wrapped around this several times so that two men could put enough friction on it to pull in a log. Then they used a horse to drag the line back out into the woods again to hook on to the next log. The "haulback" line had not been invented. Louis got Bill to bring this thing down to Savary, and between them they started a small logging operation in the bay about one mile east of Indian Point, right where the springs were, and still are.

The little donkey puffed away and dragged the logs out to the top of the bank, and then with the horse and peaveys they rolled the log down the bank and onto the beach. I remember Jimmy Anderson, Louis' eldest son, showing me just where the donkey had sat, and where they dragged the trees out. The area was not extensive and I wouldn't think they put in more than four or five sections, but this was the first real attempt to log Savary. The last time I saw Bill Palmer was in 1957 where he was still operating a small logging camp up Okeover Arm. He must have been at least seventy-five then, and still jumping across the boom in caulk boots.

The next development was when the Jenkins Logging Company bought the whole island, just for the timber rights, and started logging in about 1909. They first logged the east end of the island. They used two donkey engines and the Lord only knows how many men. Again, my information comes from the Anderson family, who were there at the time. The first donkey was a big one for its time—a ten-by-twelve two-drum Hamilton roader. It had a

wide-face main drum capable of holding up to one mile of 1⅛-inch cable with over two miles of half-inch haulback on the other drum. This donkey was situated on top of a log crib weighted down with many tons of broken rock, out at about half tide mark, about two hundred feet west of the present government wharf. A logging chute or "pole-road" ran up to the top of the hill, between Colonel Herchmer's house and where the old Savary Inn used to be. Of course there were no houses then. From the top of the hill it swung gently towards the west, angling right across the island to the south side, which we called the First Meadows. Wherever the road took a turn they would use a huge "stump roller" which was chopped into and spiked to a stump to guide the line. This logging chute or pole road was over three-quarters of a mile long, and out at the end was the other donkey, a nine-by-ten two-drum Vancouver, which was used as a yarder.

They finished this up in a year or less, and then moved the whole show up to the other end of the island and set up a similar arrangement right where Bill Palmer had been at the Springs. Their old blacksmith shop there was built of split cedar boards and shakes, and stood for many years. It was used by many people as a temporary residence. I think you can still find old bits of iron bar and rusty steel cable buried in the ground there. Down at the wharf, the old "Donkey Stand," as we called the log crib, was there for years before it rotted away, and shows as a main feature in many old photographs. One of Dad's first jobs when we came to the island in 1913 was to pry out, saw up, and burn all the old chute

Savary Island.

2

Working the steam donkey; an 11-by-14 Washington.

logs to make a garden for Colonel Herchmer, and eventually carry all the broken rock from the crib up to the garden to build the extensive rockeries that still exist. Everybody said there wouldn't be any more logging on Savary. That was the end. But times and log prices change all such predictions.

During World War I there was a lively demand for logs and the buyers weren't too fussy. Captain George Ashworth, one of the original partners in the Savary Island Syndicate, had acquired a block of property from the Jenkins estate, just west of the wharf. On the property were some trees that the former operation had not bothered with. Trees make logs, logs make money. Captain Ashworth was not one to overlook such an opportunity, and apparently most of the pieces were at hand to complete the puzzle. Louis Anderson was a logger and would know how to go about it. Harry Keefer claimed to hold a valid steam engineer's ticket so, theoretically, could run a donkey. Bill Mace was handy with tools, including an axe, and could be taught by Louis to fall trees. My dad had similar expertise and was used for hard work. All that was lacking was a steam donkey. The rest of the ingredients were instantly available, willing, and in fact desperately in need of any kind of work.

So the captain undertook to go to Vancouver and get a steam donkey. He had no more money than any of the rest, and to this day I don't know how he swung it, but in no time at all a tug and scow arrived with an imposing-looking steam donkey on board. Actually it was rather on the small side, more like what you would see on a steam pile driver of those days, but with one main difference. It had a very weird looking main drum. It was spool-shaped, like a yo-yo — small in the middle and tapering up to the ends. Apparently it had been used by the Greater Vancouver Waterworks Branch to haul a dredge bucket backwards and forwards across First Narrows before they had buried the first water pipeline to Capilano. This worked on an endless cable which just passed around the centre of the drum with about four turns, like a capstan, then looped around a block on the far side of First Narrows.

Louis Anderson looked at this thing, pushed his hat back, scratched his head, and said something unkind, partly in Swedish. The unflappable Captain Ashworth simply said that was the best he could do without any money and they better make the best of it, and would Keefer please get off his butt and drag it ashore, the tug and scow were costing money he didn't have. Now came the test. Could old man Keefer really run the thing? He puffed out his chest and assured "Bull of the Woods" Louis that he would take over just as soon as someone provided him with some water for the boiler, and enough wood to build a fire in it. So Bill Mace set about running a pipeline up to the nearest well and Dad set about beachcombing and splitting a cord of wood. In the meantime Louis struggled with the coils of rusty old used cable

to rig a block purchase from a tree on the shore, so the donkey could pull itself off as soon as Keefer got steam up.

After much puffing and snorting the little donkey pulled itself ashore and up to the foot of the hill, but only with great difficulty. It seemed to be suffering from an acute case of asthma. Foam was coming out of the exhaust instead of steam, and the engine had no power. The water they had pumped from the nearest well had too much salt in it, and this caused foaming, which can become dangerous in a steam engine. If too much foam gets in the cylinders it causes extreme water-hammering and the cylinder heads can be blown off. They eventually had to blow all the water out of the boiler and fetch more water from another well, which was farther back from the beach and had less salt content. Eventually they laid a pipeline all the way from the well and pumphouse which supplied the Savary Inn, and this in itself was quite an undertaking.

Then there was another problem. The little donkey did not have enough power to pull itself up to the top of the hill, in spite of all the luffs and blocks that old Louis Anderson could devise, so they had to grade a roadway slanting up the hill and put cross-skids on it. Dad did most of that work himself. He was always good with a shovel. Then, under old Louis' instructions, they constructed a magnificent logging chute from the beach to the top of the hill. It was over two hundred feet long, and was supported on a cribwork of logs about twenty feet above ground in the centre span. It must have contained more thousands of board feet of good fir logs than they ever put in the water. After many long weeks of work the chute was finished, the road up the hill was built, and the little donkey was moved into place to start logging.

In those days the method used was "ground yarding." The two hundred-foot spar tree and the death-defying highrigger who later came to symbolize the romance of coast logging had not even been invented yet. This shows just how much of a throwback I really am. When I first came on the scene the log was simply pulled along the surface of the ground by brute force, digging itself into the sandy ground and collecting all the limbs and branches along the way, until the donkey stalled. This would get Louis Anderson very mad, and he used language that none of us had ever heard before. In all the years we had known Louis, he had never used any bad language. He was normally very quiet, and when he did speak it was always in great deference to his listeners. He had come over from Sweden as a grown man and still had difficulty with the English language, which made him a bit self-conscious. He was also a very gentle and patient man. No one was prepared for the complete change wrought by his being suddenly elevated to the position of hooktender and woods boss of the G & K Logging Company, as the locals were now calling the outfit (but not when George and Kate Ashworth were listening). He under-

Greg "Sharkey" Palmer going up.

went an amazing transformation just as soon as he put on his new pair of Leckie's caulk boots, bought for the occasion. (He was the only one with proper logging boots. No one else could afford them.) At the slightest provocation, he would switch to extremely bad language and become uncharacteristically fluent. His eyes blazed and foam appeared at the corners of his mouth, causing him to spit tobacco juice between each flood of obscenity, all of which added drama to the moment.

For instance, whenever the little donkey engine got stuck, and the crew had to rally around and "fight the hang-up," this would precipitate an immediate outburst from Louis. On some occasions he would throw his hat on the ground and jump up and down on it with his caulk boots while he said the most unkind things about the little donkey, which he claimed "couldn't pull a limp dick out of a lard pail." Then he would switch to the subject of Harry Keefer, who was well out of earshot, dwelling on the size of Keefer's belly and his ineptitude as a "donkey puncher." There was undoubtedly some substance to his complaints, but it didn't make the job any easier for the crew. It was very hard work. They would saw and chop the logs, limbs, and branches out of the way, and then even resort to manpower with peaveys and pries to assist the donkey to get the log moving again. It was very slow work.

As kids we would run up the hill right after school to watch the fun, usually getting cursed and told to "Get the hell outta the way!" On one or two occasions we sneaked up there during the long evenings after the crew had gone home. We had it all to ourselves out of earshot from the closest habitation, and if there was still a little steam pressure left in the boiler, Jimmy Anderson, one of Louis' many sons, would climb up on the machine and run the engine very carefully—chuffa clank—chuffa clank—chuffa clank—wheeze clankety clank. We would hook the choker onto an old slab of a log and haul it slowly out with the haulback, and then back in to the donkey again. Two or three of us would ride on it, and Jimmy would handle the engine. He had been a whistle punk in his uncles' camp up at Stuart Island during school holidays, so he knew all about these things. We would run it till there was no steam left. It was tremendous fun. We knew enough not to blow the whistle and attract attention.

I don't remember how long they operated, or how much timber they put in the water, but it was not enough to pay wages and the whole thing ground to a halt. The little donkey sat up there by itself for quite a time, just getting rustier and rustier. G & K was finished. Eventually Sealskin Norton, a well-known character in the coastal logging scene, bought the donkey. He arrived with a scow and a tug and an engineer. He really did wear an ankle-length brown sealskin coat and a fur hat even though it was then summertime. They threw a fire in the donkey and started to move it to the scow, but this engineer

immediately detected something was not right. The engine had no power. He got out his tools and carefully readjusted the valve settings. A few minutes later he opened the throttle and the little donkey practically leaped off the ground. I have often wondered if the logging operation might have turned out differently if this malfunction had been detected and corrected earlier, but on the other hand we might never have learned so many swear words. The site of the old logging chute was about half a mile along the shore to the west of the government dock, close to where Major Stevens built a log cabin on stilts. It remained there for many years, standing as a monument to enterprise and optimism, if nothing else.

All was quiet on the logging front for about two years, and then, in 1917, George Verdi and A.P. Allison arrived, unannounced, with two very large horses. One was black and the other was brown. They went up to the Springs and used the old blacksmith shop as headquarters. Their actual logging operation took place about half a mile east of the spring. They built a rollway where the bank is only about forty feet high, and then an old-fashioned skid road that meandered back across the island almost to the south shore. All they were after was fir piling—straight trees about forty to sixty feet long and about twelve inches on the top. This kind of logging did not scar the countryside very badly, and in fact it was hard to see where they had actually been cutting. They were only a few months doing it. They disappeared as quietly as they had come, but left the two horses to fend for themselves for a year or more. They stayed mostly on the meadows on the south side of the island where Captain Ashworth once had the grass golf course. The old horses were very docile and good natured and used to wander down to our end of the island sometimes. They always walked side by side, as they had when they were a team hauling logs. In my last year of school I looked out the old schoolhouse window and saw those two horses, one black, the other brown, walking side by side along the front with about four or five kids perched on the back of each horse, whacking them with their hands and trying to get them to race. I thought this was extremely funny and I giggled and got hell from the teacher. On a sadder note, one of the horses took a tumble down the cliff and broke his leg and died. Verdi and Allison eventually came back to get the remaining one, who was getting very lonely.

There were to be other attempts at logging Savary over the years but, like most island enterprises, they would prove futile. No doubt this was due in some part to the grade of timber that was taken off. The main crop was fir. Old growth fir, but of very slow growth, and poor quality. A very large percentage was very "conky." This might not be apparent from the ground, but after felling and bucking, large areas of internal damage would be exposed. My father and I depended largely for a number of years

Team of logging horses, Gibsons.

on felling and cutting fir trees for firewood in many parts of Savary, and often we would take down a likely-looking tree, only to find that less than 50 percent was usable even for firewood. It is an interesting fact that the disease of fir trees known in the industry as conk was apparently unknown to the old-timers, and was only noticed and identified after the turn of the century. Experts tell us that it was a disease originating in the Orient and brought in by the white man. On this subject I am a little out of my depth, but I can tell you that many times we would find very old windfalls that had been lying on the ground and covered in moss for over fifty years, and they never, but never, were conky. Usually sound as a bell inside, with only the sap and bark rotted.

Marianas Mars *in service camouflage.*

the GENTLE GIANTS of Sproat Lake

A.M. FEAST

CONVERTING THE WORLD'S LARGEST operational flying boats into fire-fighting water bombers wasn't easy. Presumably the US Forestry Service knew something; when offered the surplus fleet by the US Navy, they turned it down flat. Later, when those brash Canadians proposed to not only modify the aircraft but operate them over the mountainous terrain of British Columbia, the whole idea, in the considered opinion of some experts, was downright batty.

That was back in 1959 and for a while, admittedly, the skeptics seemed to have a point. The problems that bedeviled the operation during the first two years were daunting. But the Forest Industries Flying Tankers Limited, a consortium of six BC forestry companies, persevered. Now, over thirty years later, the Martin Mars are still flying, sluicing out forest fires with a youthful verve that belies their venerable air-frames. Their flight crews are properly respectful of their charges, as well they should be. After all, the Mars were spanning the Pacific long before most members of the flight crews were born. The men's pride in their aircraft and the vital role they are fulfilling in BC is apparent as they guide visitors around the main company base at Sproat Lake, some eight kilometres northwest of Port Alberni on Vancouver Island. During the past two and a half decades the aerial tankers have saved the province and industry multi-millions of dollars in timber losses and fire prevention costs.

The late Glenn Martin would undoubtedly be pleased too, if somewhat bemused. Forest fire suppression was far from his objective when he first presented his design for a large patrol bomber in 1937. The legendary aviation pioneer, designer, and builder finally sold his concept to the US Navy and in August 1938 his company was awarded the contract for a prototype, some $8 million being allocated for it by Congress.

Designated as type X-PB2M-1, the twin-ruddered, four-engined flying boat was launched on November 8, 1941, made its maiden flight on June 23, 1942, and then, after completing all test requirements, was delivered to Naval Squadron VR-2 at Alameda Air Station in California. By then its role as patrol bomber had been discarded and the machine was to serve as a general purpose transport. During its operational life, X-PB2M-1 set new long distance and cargo-lifting service records. Her flight characteristics, seaworthiness, and general ease of maintenance earned the Martin machine the affectionate sobriquet of "The Old Lady" on VR-2 squad-

ron. Spurred by her success, the US Navy contracted for eighteen machines in 1944, to be officially designated as type JRM 1. The Mars was to differ from the prototype in that it featured a single rudder and larger fuel capacity, one permitting a 5,000-mile range. The cost of the aircraft was tabled at $3.5 million each. Then, in 1945 with the war drawing palpably to a close, the Martin order was reduced to six machines.

The first production aircraft caught fire over Chesapeake Bay while on a test flight in August 1945. The crew landed it safely but were helpless to arrest the fire that consumed the flying boat in the water. The second plane was delivered to VR-2 squadron in early 1946 and the remaining four were produced and delivered during the next two years. The navy, in deference to the squadron's transport role in the south Pacific theatre, and in remembrance of past campaigns, named each flying boat after a south Pacific island group or archipelago. The names were emblazoned high on their respective bows: *Marianas*, *Philippine*, *Hawaii*, *Marshall*, and *Caroline Mars*.

During the years 1948–1953, the Mars fleet averaged five weekly round trips across the Pacific, carrying personnel, material, and general supplies. From late 1953 through 1956, they provided a reduced thrice-weekly trans-Pacific service. Routinely, the Mars established new service records. On May 19, 1949 the *Marianas Mars* took one load of 301 navy personnel to her capacious bosom and ferried them from Alameda to San Diego. A routine supply

Like feisty dowagers – Philippine *and* Hawaii Mars.

9

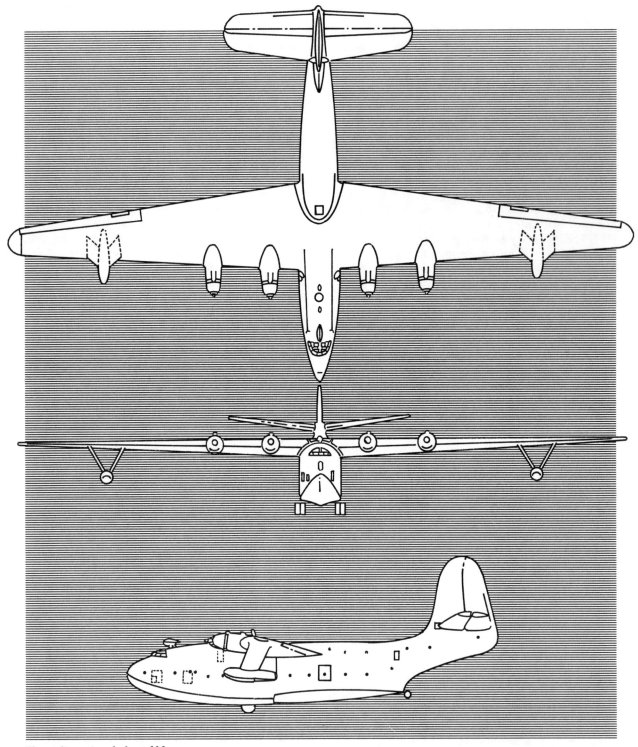

Three-dimensional plan of Mars.

run established a new weight-lifting record with a load of 68,327 pounds. The *Marshall Mars* suffered an in-flight fire off Honolulu on April 5, 1950 but landed safely on the sea. The fire forced the crew to abandon the plane and she was lost. In their ten years of operation, the Mars fleet logged 87,000 otherwise accident-free hours.

Meanwhile, north of the 49th Parallel, records of quite a different kind were impinging on the balance sheets of British Columbia's forest industry. In the mid-50s, a series of disastrous forest fires struck the province during the dry summer months. Timber losses and fire fighting costs soared to a level that finally prompted the industry giant, MacMillan Bloedel, to call an emergency meeting in 1958 of all lumber companies. A Fire Protection Committee was formed and charged with conducting a reappraisal of all existing ground and air defence systems. This was to be followed by a comprehensive report incorporating recommended changes.

"Like a block of flats."

The committee's main finding pinpointed the inadequacy of the aircraft currently being used in water bombing. Although a mix of waterborne, amphibious, and land-based civilian and ex-service planes were being used, all were deemed deficient in one or more key areas.

Dan McIvor, a committee member and at that time Mac Blo's senior executive pilot, spelled out the all-too-familiar scenario of rampant fires in the 1950s. "Given dry, tinderly forest conditions," he explained, "a newly ignited fire can spread over an area of five acres within fifteen minutes. If not contained before this critical point and even in calm wind conditions, the blaze can become a raging inferno beyond any immediate hope of checking it." Such outbreaks had to be hit early and hard with massive floods of water. All too often they were started by lightning strikes in remote areas of the province. By the time aircraft could appear on the scene with their inadequate water loads the fire was out of control. Whatever the merits of single-engined Beavers, Otters, Grumman Avengers and the amphibious Canso in the forestry services of other provinces, they lacked, in the opinion of McIvor, the speed, the range, and above all the water load capacity to deal effectively with major fire outbreaks in the vast coniferous forests of BC.

McIvor decided to conduct a search for more effective aircraft. The tall, bespectacled pilot, then in his early thirties, had a broad background of bush flying experience, including five years with the BC Forest Service. He had long been convinced that only very large flying boats or amphibians would fulfill the need.

The dogged search started but by early 1959 it was increasingly obvious that McIvor was scouring the aircraft marts of the world for types that no longer existed or were unavailable. The era of the great flying boats was past, or so it seemed. BOAC advised that their Princess boats were retired, their engines in total disrepair. Pan Am reported that their famed pre-war Clippers had all been wrecked in service. The Boeing Clipper, the Short Sunderland, the Martin Mariner, the Tornado, the Martin Clipper — all were either no longer in existence, or no longer flyable. And then, late in the spring of 1959, a chance remark made by an old bush flying acquaintance of Dan McIvor triggered renewed hope.

"I hear," said Bob Morin, "that the American Navy are selling off their Martin Mars in California." This casual observation immediately prompted a flurry of phone calls by McIvor. Finally he made contact with the official Navy spokesman at Alameda Air Station, near San Francisco.

Dan McIvor.

The officer's remarks were trenchant and seemed to dash any hopes. Yes, the Mars fleet had been declared surplus. The aircraft were out to public tender, one of which, coincidentally, closed on the morrow. No, a further bid could not be accepted. Yes, he would advise the caller in due course of the name of the successful bidder.

A week later Dan McIvor was at the naval station in Alameda staring at four Martin Mars beached like so many stranded whales on the concrete slipways. He was accompanied by a management representative from Mac Blo and two engineers from Fairey Aviation. Earlier, McIvor's navy contact had informed him that the winning bid had been submitted by a Mr. Hugo Forrester of the Mars Metals Company, a scrap metal outfit. Mac Blo acceded to McIvor's importunities to the extent of authorizing an inspection team. They were to inspect the aircraft, review all relevant details then return and report.

Accompanied by Forrester, the Canadians pored over the four machines, shaking their heads in respectful awe. The Mars has an overall length of 120 feet, a hull beam of 13 feet 5 inches, and a hull draft of 5 feet 5 inches. It has a wing length of 200 feet with four 18-cylinder Wright Cyclone engines each rated at 2,400 hp, driving 4-bladed Curtis Electric propellers with a diameter of 15 feet 2 inches. The single rudder soars 44 feet. The 35-foot control cabin or flight deck resembled a studio apartment, or so it seemed on first appraisal by the Canadians. The fleet had been withdrawn from service in 1956, still wore their dull service camouflage, and, despite having been in a de-commissioned state for three years, appeared to be in mint condition. There were distinct overtones of a grade B Hollywood scenario in what followed next.

Forrester's successful bid had been in the exact amount of $23,650, or slightly less than the cost of majoring one used Wright Cyclone engine. For this munificent sum he had fallen heir to four intact flying boats, or in scrap metal terms some 324 short tons of produce at a cost of $73 a ton. It further developed that Mars Metals Company had a cash flow problem; in fact the winning bid had been made with borrowed money. Mr. Forrester would be pleased to sell all or part of his Mars fleet to the Canadian interests.

Upon his return to Head Office, McIvor hastily compiled the team's findings and submitted a brief glowing report to Mac Blo management, a report that concluded with a strong recommendation to purchase the four machines immediately. He then sat back expectantly to await Head Office's laudatory remarks and approval to proceed with purchase negotiations. Forrester had hinted broadly that his thinking ran to $25,000 per plane. Management mulled over the McIvor report, gave it a cursory review—and turned the whole project down.

An utterly deflated McIvor moped around for days. The decision was incomprehensible. Where had he gone wrong? Now Forrester would have to be told that the deal was off. Still he delayed, draped morosely over his desk. A visiting salesman acquaintance dropped in, noted the forlorn figure, and inquired about the nature of his problem. McIvor poured out his tale of woe.

"Is it still a good deal?" asked the sales type.

"The best," groaned McIvor, "but we're going to lose it."

"Naturally," replied the visitor, wise in the mores of bureaucracy, "unless you go back after 'em again—but this time with a proper report."

With hope flickering again, McIvor enlisted the aid of a company accountant and together they toiled over an expanded presentation. For ten consecutive nights they drafted and re-drafted a detailed report, one replete with graphs, charts, projections, cost analyses—the works. When it was done, he resubmitted it to Head Office, which accepted it non-committally. Then he waited. And waited.

Meanwhile, back at Alameda there was a time factor involved in the removal of the Mars from the station, a pressure that exacerbated McIvor's sleepless nights. All planes had to be off the station six months from tender date. However, the first had to be removed within 90 days, the second by 30 days thereafter, the third 30 days after that, the fourth 30 days after that. A month had already passed since Forrester had taken title. Mac Blo remained mute and McIvor could do nothing.

McIvor finally phoned Forrester and, in a voice brimming with false confidence, asked if, pending a few minor details being resolved in BC, one machine could be placed in the water and towed across the bay to the shore of the San Francisco municipal airport. The Californian, obviously cheered by this indication of an imminent sale, readily agreed. There was little cheer for Dan McIvor, however, as he sweated out the company decision.

Finally the decision was handed down. After serious reconsideration, Mac Blo had elected to purchase the four aircraft on behalf of an industry consortium yet to be formed. McIvor, accompanied by an air engineer, was dispatched to Alameda to conclude negotiations. Terms of the sale were $100,000 for the four machines, with the vendor guaranteeing to bring all aircraft up to an airworthy, ferryable state.

Shortly thereafter a further government tender was opened, this time offering some thirty-five surplus Wright Cyclone engines and spares from the Mars inventory. McIvor moved to bid for the lot but was restrained by Mac Blo and told to settle for six. The bid of $135 each was successful. (At a later date, McIvor pursued the other twenty-nine power plants which had ended up in the hands of a New York scrap dealer. They were purchased for $600 each.) The Canadian bid successfully for 5,000 spark plugs at 5 cents each and a number of new unused cylinder heads and cylinders for $15 apiece.

By mid-July a scurrying Dan McIvor had become a familiar sight to station personnel as he sped around the big air base on myriad errands. Even though he talked American funny, they warmed to the friendly Canadian pilot for he was the key mover in saving their esteemed Mars from the ignominy of the scrap yard. He was trying to keep them flying and for that alone he deserved their interest and support. And how he was to need it! Mac Blo, now busily engaged in the formation of Forest Industries Flying Tankers Limited, had stipulated that all four machines be flown to BC — a sweeping enjoiner that tended to overlook such harsh facts as the lack of qualified flight crews, thorough aircraft maintenance checks, ferry permits, and a host of other complexities.

Prominent among McIvor's Alameda contacts and well-wishers was the station supply officer. He had sized up the Canadians' problem and moved adroitly to ameliorate it. He enlisted the services of a senior ex-captain of the Martin Mars, a Lieutenant Commander Maloney who agreed, during off-duty hours, to check out McIvor on the type. Also conjured up was a Chief Petty Officer Traxler, an ex-Mars flight engineer who stood ready not only to vet the work of the Canadian engineer trainee, but to act as liaison between naval ground technicians and McIvor. The Canadian had but to say the word, guarantee the pay, and all would be taken care of.

A vastly relieved and delighted McIvor was thus introduced to the fine old tradition of moonlighting, and blessed the military five-day work week. In the midst of a growing flurry of activity on the four aircraft he was accosted by the squadron engineer-ing officer in charge of surplus equipment. "Say, Dan," he said, "I've found some more parts: you interested?" McIvor nodded with alacrity and was led to a secluded area of the base until they came to a halt beside a stacked pile of opened and unopened crates. They lay in a column 20 feet wide, 10 feet high and close to 200 feet long.

"Which ones?" queried McIvor.

"All of 'em," replied the officer laconically.

McIvor gulped and essayed a superficial examination of the pile. It appeared to be composed of an incredible pot-pourri of hydraulics, transfer motors, pumps, cable, control surfaces, beaching gear, in fact the whole remaining Mars equipment inventory.

"How...how much would we have to pay for them?" he heard himself saying meekly.

"What do you think they're worth?" responded the officer.

The Canadian mumbled something about it not being a matter of what they were worth, but how much they could afford to pay.

"Make us an offer," the navy minion said encouragingly.

Dollar figures pinwheeled in McIvor's head. Each seemed to have a glowering Mac Blo executive lurking behind it, reacting to yet another unauthorized McIvor ploy. Finally, "How about $3,200?" he ventured.

The officer gazed at the Canadian for a moment, then said, "You know, there's two and a half million bucks in this pile." McIvor shuffled his feet and gazed across the bay. The officer drummed absently on a wooden crate for a moment then drew himself erect. "Well, OK for now," he said briskly. "You realize of course that regulations require that we solicit a minimum of three public bids. We'll give you one invitation and this afternoon I'll send one each to approved dealers in New York and Florida. Then I'll close the bids tomorrow." As he glanced at the Canadian there was a slight tremor in one of his eyelids that could be interpreted as a wink.

Later that week McIvor was hosted by the squadron engineering office, which introduced him to a solid phalanx of filing cabinets. "Yours, we believe," beamed a spokesman. The guest blinked at forty-three metal cabinets crammed with Mars memorabilia: documents, files, mechanical drawings, maintenance records, the entire technical history built up during a decade of Mars service. As a final touch, a large grey metal cabinet was added to the store. It was the repository of complete sets of templates covering the hull sections. (These were to prove invaluable in the early 1970s when the thinning, leaking hulls had to replaced in a complex alclad repair scheme.) A now somewhat dazed McIvor, forced to don yet another hat, went looking for the next BC-bound freighter to convey the mound of parts and technical records.

On August 8, 1959 it all came together. The *Marianas Mars* lifted from a foaming one-mile takeoff

Dawn on Sproat Lake.

run up the bay. Her engines booming a triumphant farewell, she dipped a wing in salute to Alameda and set course northwards. Hours later she settled complacently in the waters of Patricia Bay. The crew handed her over to Fairey Aviation and returned to San Francisco. On August 27 the *Caroline Mars* joined her at Patricia Bay. The ferry operation had functioned smoothly and again the crew returned by air to Alameda.

The *Philippine Mars* thundered down the bay early in the morning of September 5 and lifted into her northbound flight, well ahead of schedule. She was cruising comfortably off the Oregon coast when it happened. Her four engines cut out and eighty-one tons of flying boat slid like a winged brick towards the heaving Pacific Ocean. There was a high overcast and a whipping wind reflected by whitecapped waves.

"The silence was pretty deafening," said Dan McIvor some twenty-six years later, "and as luck would have it, I had earlier vacated my co-pilot's seat and was roaming around below in the cargo department." Coincidentally, the navy flight engineer had left his control panel to visit the head. McIvor stumbled down the steep catwalk of the cavernous hull, then sped up the spiral stairs to the flight deck, just in time to collide with Traxler scrambling back to his post. They clawed their way back to their respective seats, past a frozen Canadian engineer trainee whose unskilled fiddling at the console had cut off all fuel to the engines.

The hands of the American crewman flew over his panel. "Feather number one," he bellowed over the intercom to a baffled captain in the left seat. Then, "Feather number two—feather number three." As the windmilling screws slowed, then locked, the captain, wrestling with the flying controls, drawled a martyred, "Come on Traxler, leave me one, will ya."

The craft had been cruising at 10,000 feet when the engines died. "Thank heavens that we had the height," reflected McIvor ruefully, "for we were to need all of it. Those waves seemed to grow larger by the second." Both pilots applied vise-like grips to the sluggish dual control columns, while thirty feet behind them a sweating engineer juggled with fuel cocks, pitch controls, starter switches, and throttles. The altimeter wound down. Then slowly, one by one, the engines coughed, spat, and spun the four-bladed propellers. The flying boat arced slowly out of the dive, scant feet above the tossing whitecaps. A pale and chastened crew reset course for Vancouver Island.

Late in the afternoon of September 12, the *Hawaii Mars* banked over Pat Bay, then landed in a welter of foam. She taxied in to moor beside her three sister ships. Two weary Americans departed for home after a job superbly done. The newly formed Flying Tankers, chief pilot Dan McIvor, bade them a grateful farewell. There was to be little

Flight engineers at work.

respite for the fledgling company before facing the next series of hurdles.

The *Caroline Mars* was flown to the new base at Sproat Lake. Here the ground crews and flight personnel would receive their first indoctrination. As the sole qualified pilot for the type, Dan McIvor would have to shoulder all pilot training. A retired senior ex-Royal Canadian Air Force officer had been named general manager of the company and on his own initiative hired the first staff pilot. The man was an ex-service pilot with extensive multi-engine experience but no apparent bush flying or fire-fighting background. McIvor had little time to worry about that as he plunged into a detailed training syllabus for all hands at the base. Meanwhile the *Marianas Mars* had been drawn ashore atop her beaching gear and hangared by Fairey Aviation Limited, awaiting her modification to water bomber. In late autumn all ground and flying training exercises ceased and the *Caroline* was flown back to Patricia Bay.

During the winter months the Fairey technical staff, working in conjunction with Flying Tankers' engineers, stripped the interior of the *Marianas*, removing insulation, panelling, passenger seats and all other extraneous fittings, preparatory to the water tank installation. The Department of Transport, Aviation Branch, were involved and very supportive during the planning and execution of the aircraft modification. A single 6,000-gallon fibreglassed Douglas fir plywood tank was designed and installed by sections in the cargo compartment of the hull. Two four-foot square dumping hatches were cut on either side of the hull and linked to the tank. Two retractable probes or scoops were faired in just aft of the hull step. New radio equipment was installed, and

Up front — pilot and co-pilot.

the exterior of the aircraft was painted in the company's red and white colour scheme.

Following a number of shakedown flights that spring of 1960, the *Marianas* was flown to Sproat Lake for continued training. It was fortunate that a soporific Mother Nature elected to free the island forests of major fire outbreaks that summer. McIvor and company were soon head to head with Murphy's Law and serviceability problems. They may have resulted from pure perverseness on the part of the Mars, or her surly reaction to the ministrations of still inexperienced ground crews; whatever the reason, the result was a crimped flying program. Engines went out, then propellers; pumps didn't; electrics failed and tempers flared. When she flew, and the trainee flight crews got over their initial intimidation, they found their work cut out for them on the flight deck.

When the craft is airborne, the command pilot is fully engrossed in operating the flying and trim controls only. The massive 60-foot ailerons are not servo or power-assisted and to function require solid muscle power from the pilot. The flight engineer and air mechanic, seated side by side at the control console some thirty feet aft of the pilots' compartment, operate the throttles and pitch and mixture controls in response to the captain's verbal commands over the intercom. The co-pilot monitors the captain and assists him on the flying controls if required. When taxiing on the water, the captain assumes power control from the cockpit throttle quadrant which is duplicated at the engineer's post. The two crewmen must constantly scan all gauges and instruments on their panel, while ministering to the demands of the four power plants and riding herd on a complex of switches governing fuel flow,

◆◆

Modifying the bird was complex. When it was built, each had 7½ miles of wiring, 3,000,000 rivets, 60,000 lbs. of aluminum, 25,000 lbs. of steel, 1.9 miles of conduit and piping, 800 sq. ft. of plywood, 750 lbs. of rubber, 800 lbs. of plastic, 650 cubic yards of fabric and a mixed ton of copper, tin, and zinc. And let's not omit 300 gallons of paint.

✦

The flight deck alone is larger than the entire cabin area of a DC-3. The JRM-1 cruised at 137 kts,

the JRM-2 at 150 kts. Maximum speeds were 192 kts. and 206 kts. respectively.

✦

Caroline Mars was the last to be produced but reigned as first among equals. She had been fitted with bigger engines, the P & W 3,000 hp giving her an enhanced speed, range, and gross weight capability. She was nominated as the JRM-2, the only one of the series built.

electronics, compressors, hydraulics, and pumps. To facilitate manoeuvring on the water, both outboard engines are fitted with reverse pitch propellers.

When the instructor was reasonably satisfied with his students' proficiency in circuits and bumps, they progressed to water tank filling exercises. Learning this called for a nicety of speed control that was to cost a number of pricey hand-crafted stainless steel scoops before it was mastered. The Mars lands at 74 knots. It must then be checked and held in the high "step" at 72 knots, a speed that trial and error dictated was the optimum for the safe lowering of the scoops or probes into the relatively undisturbed water just aft of the rear chine. When this manoeuvre is properly executed, the water surges into the 6,000-gallon tank and fills it in 26 seconds. Then the probes are immediately retracted, the throttles are cracked open, and the plane becomes airborne after a brief takeoff run. Failure to maintain these filling conditions can lead to damage or even destruction of the probes.

Sporadic serviceability problems continued to bedevil the flying training and it was autumn before the first simulated fire suppression sorties were possible. Although there was no precedent governing the operation of a ponderous flying boat as a close-in water bomber, McIvor elected to follow the time-proven aerial fire control tactics employing a "bird dog" spotter plane linked by radio to both water bombers and the ground controller "fire boss." The controller is in overall charge of both ground and air fire-fighting crews; the spotter plane acts as his aerial surveillance and relays his radioed instructions. In practice sessions with the Mars, the "bird dog" machine was given the additional responsibility of determining the bomber's final flight path over the target area, a course that safety dictates must always be down and away from high terrain and clear of obstructions.

Mac Blo's Grumman Goose amphibian was the *Marianas'* mentor during her first simulated "callout" sorties that autumn. This was to prove the most critical and dangerous phase of the training: guiding the heavily loaded craft over high ranges, down valleys and canyons, and low over serried stands of dense forest. As their experience increased, the pilots found that maximum ground saturation was achieved when the drop was made at an air speed of 100 knots, and at a height varying from 150 to 200 feet. At times buffeted by swirling winds, flying low, and with control sluggish at slow speed, it was no theatre for the unwary. When the Mars jettisoned its 30-ton load, the surging wave blanketed an area of three to four acres. Viewed from the ground, it was a spectacular sight. Then, her bow lifting and her dumping hatches closing, the Mars flew to the nearest body of water capable of sustaining her skimming, tank-recharging run.

In April of 1961 Dan McIvor was dealt a devastating blow. The Department of Transport advised, on the basis of McIvor's last bi-annual medical examination, that his corrective lenses were no longer

The "scoops."

Indefatigable bird-dog — the Grumman Goose.

acceptable. A newly appointed chief medical officer was wielding a heavy broom and although McIvor's vision with glasses was unimpaired, the thickness of lenses necessary to achieve it was unacceptable. In effect his pilot's licence would be invalidated.

McIvor was shattered and the company was in a quandary. Some three co-pilots were advanced in training but none were at a captaincy level at this stage. Then an understanding DOT offered a solution. The Flying Tankers chief pilot would be granted a three-week grace period before his licence was cancelled, in order to allow sufficient time for completion of the captaincy training.

The general manager immediately pressed McIvor to concentrate on his protégé and to expedite his qualifying check-out. It was plain that this man would shortly be assuming the role of chief pilot. McIvor complied and pushed the flight training hard during late April and May. The ex-service pilot performed with average competence while in the left seat, but McIvor was secretly concerned about the man's overt signs of stress in the air, such as his heavy sweating. Nevertheless, e was deemed qualified at the end of May and continued practising with his own crew. They had their first callout on the morning of June 23, a relatively minor outbreak north of the base. The aircraft experienced engine trouble and they returned to base. Airborne again after repairs, the *Marianas* arrived over the scene in the late morning to find that the outbreak had been largely contained by ground fire-fighting crews. The Mars made a single token drop.

That afternoon another fire alert had the same crew in the air within twenty minutes, speeding to a major fire some thirty kilometres west of Nanaimo. The fire was centred in a bowl-like depression halfway up a mountain spur behind which stood high, jagged peaks. The "bird dog" plane was already on the scene awaiting the bomber. The Mars appeared rounding the flank of the mountain and then, seemingly oblivious of the guide plane, altered course and flew directly towards the smoke-filled depression. Startled watchers in the air and on the ground saw the climbing bomber breast the spur, skim the treeline, and continue across the bowl tracking into higher terrain. No water drop was seen. Then the onlookers saw the port wing of the machine drop suddenly in the start of a steep turn. The next moment the wingtip struck a tree and the horrified witnesses watched the Mars cartwheel and crash. There were no survivors.

"What happened, Dan?" the president of Mac Blo asked bluntly the next day. McIvor had flown over the crash site, retraced that final fateful course, and arrived at the inescapable conclusion.

"It was pilot error," he said.

Management moved quickly. The *Caroline Mars* was ordered into service and McIvor was named general manager of Forest Industries Flying Tankers Limited. Another decision was made as a result of the June 23 tragedy. W.F. "Bill" Waddington, who was to succeed McIvor as general manager, spelled it out in an interview in July of 1981. "We also established," he said, "that the absolute minimum

18

Going down—6,000 gallons worth.

W.F. "Bill" Waddington.

flying qualification acceptable for tanker pilot applicants would be 7,000 hours of BC coastal and mountain flying experience, preferably on float-equipped or amphibious planes."

The Mars operated for the rest of the 1961 season on a month-to-month trial basis. There was a tacit understanding that any further major setbacks would spell quietus to the grand experiment. The callouts were frequent but the fires were minor in scope and readily stamped out, frequently in conjunction with ground fire crews. Dan McIvor, his pilot's licence reinstated after an appeal, saw the fire season draw to a close with the gnawing feeling that the aircraft's full potential had yet to be tested.

In the early summer of 1962 two episodes occurred that laid the question to rest. The season began with an outbreak at the base of a steep hill rearing up from the shore of Cowichan Lake. It spread rapidly up the slope as the fire induced its own forced draft. Ground crews were still trying to break through to the site when the *Caroline Mars* appeared over the scene. She laid a flooding load across the top perimeter of the advancing conflagration, then settled in on the lake, recharged her tank, and laid the next load across the base of the fire. Six further drops were made across the face of the burning hill, moving progressively upwards. As a pugnacious Mars banked in with a ninth load, the

drop was stayed. The fire was out, totally extinguished in less than an hour. A nearby professional photographer recorded the action.

Two days later, the Mars was circling a blaze at the head of Ramsey Arm. Fresh from their exploit at Cowichan Lake, McIvor and Cal Lee looked down at a fiery, smoking outbreak that had all the earmarks of a dirty one. The fire had taken hold in massive windfalls of toppled cedars near the water's edge. Mature cedars, many of them fourteen feet in diameter, towered above the flames, their intact top boughs acting as a protective canopy. Then one by one, they started to "candle." Slowly descending, the Mars banked offshore and approached the stand of timber at an altitude lower than tree height. As it zoomed to clear the treetops, the water load was unleashed in a slingshot effect that cascaded the flood below the tree canopy and subjected the burning windfalls to the full impact of 6,000 gallons. Nearby commercial fishermen saw huge tangles of prostrate cedars jump and roll with the force of the water. After six drops, fire was no longer visible among the windfalls. McIvor and Lee next concentrated on the burning trees and further saturation of the ground area, flying low and unloading through the green umbrella. Mature trees receiving the full force of thirty tons of water snapped or were bowled over. Two hours and twenty-two drops later, the

Caroline Mars flicked her impressive tail at the thoroughly squelched forest fire and minced back to Sproat Lake at 150 knots.

Quite suddenly, the saga of the Martin Mars again became a media event. The Cowichan Lake photos and the *Caroline*'s heroic exploits had seen to that.

"Suddenly too," said Dan McIvor wryly of those days, "everybody wanted into the act." There was a plethora of memos and reports by numerous experts. As the majority shareholder in Forest Industries Flying Tankers, Mac Blo maintained firm proprietary control. McIvor's position as general manager took increasing pressure both from above and from below. The *Caroline Mars* continued to staunchly vindicate her role that summer in a series of successful callout sorties.

Hurricane Frieda struck the south coast of Vancouver Island during October 12–23, 1962. The gusting winds caught the *Caroline Mars* atop her beaching gear on Patricia Bay airport, where she was securely anchored to tie-down clamps by half-inch steel cables. During the early hours of October 13, when the gale was at its height, the straining aircraft reared and snapped one hawser. She then slewed until another was dragged through its retaining clamp. Freed, the Mars careened across the field until she struck the shoulder of the main runway. A wing lifted and the tip of the other gouged a track on the concrete before the machine crunched to earth with a squeal of rending metal. Dawn disclosed the full extent of the damage. One wingtip was crushed and folded back, the main bulkhead was cracked, the tail section was twisted. An eighteen-inch crack gaped along the full width of the hull. The *Caroline* was a write-off, fit only for spare parts.

Once again a sombre board of directors met to decide the future of the flying tankers. After minimal debate they elected to bite the bullet, and ordered conversion of the remaining two machines.

The *Philippine* and *Hawaii Mars* emerged in the spring, each with a new weapon added to her arsenal: a ten-foot high torpedo-shaped vessel standing vertically beside the main water tank. This was to contain Gelgard, a powdered thickening agent measured into the main tank as it fills with fresh water. The chemical imparts a slippery gel effect to the liquid, aids in compacting the water, and retards evaporation while coating the target area in a clinging viscous film. 1963 marked the opening of a whole new chapter in the annals of Forest Industries Flying Tankers, one that is still being written. By then, however, the man whose concept it was, and who had stamped the Mars operation with his own signature, was gone. Dan McIvor had departed for Pacific Western Airways to manage their light aircraft fleet operation, and subsequently their Hercules freighter division.

Conair's DC-6 weighs in.

21

He was succeeded by Bill Waddington, under whose long tenure as general manager the company evolved into its present lean and efficient form. In the process they welded together a taut, cohesive team of air and ground engineers, mechanics, and ten pilots, once described by an industry spokesman in a hyperbolic aside as "the world's most exclusive club of airline pilots." In 1974 the company acquired its first Bell 206 helicopter and subsequently added two more. The Grumman Goose, now nudging its fourth decade, still reigns as "bird dog." The choppers are used for communication, ambulance, and sport fires control. All six machines beam from a large measure of TLC.

To me, there is that old tingling sense of a wartime operational station permeating the Sproat Lake base during the fire season. It was Code Yellow on the Fire Danger Index board when I boarded the *Philippine Mars*. I walked the length of the cavernous hull, my footsteps on the catwalk echoing hollowly through the bulkheads, until I reached the stern and gazed upwards through the structure of that massive empennage. Retracing my steps, I went to the spiral staircase leading to the flight deck. As one emerges from the stairwell, the control console located just forward and on the port side of the cabin draws attention. Here, the flight engineer and flight mechanic, seated side by side, reign over a complex thicket of gauges, switches, and controls. Next, from the pilots' cockpit, thirty feet forward of the console, I stared out over the huge wing, the powerful engines, and shook my head in the respectful wonder incumbent upon any aging ex-twin-engined medium bomber pilot. Off the port wing tip, the *Hawaii Mars* swung

at her mooring buoy before a backdrop of shimmering water and a steeply rising shoreline. Both crews and aircraft were on a thirty-minute readiness status. A Code Red, warning of extreme fire hazard in the woods, dictates an immediate readiness state.

Tom Irving is general manager of the company now, having succeeded Bill Waddington on his retirement in the mid-1980s. As a result of recent company amalgamations, there are now only three member firms of Forest Industries Flying Tankers: MacMillan Bloedel, CIP Forest Products, and British Columbia Forest Products. Forest Industries Flying Tankers will continue to guard zealously their timber preserves on Vancouver Island and on the mainland. The flying boats are in mint condition and with an adequate stock of spares, engines, and propellers, are capable of flying indefinitely.

At the close of the 1986 season, Tom Irving obligingly compiled the statistics for me. Number of major forest fires quelled since the formation of the company—373, involving 6,479 drops. Total operational hours flown—2,160, in the course of which some 33,826,700 Imperial gallons were dropped.

Once known as the Queens of the South Pacific, the two hardy survivors of that once regal flight now reign as feisty dowagers, militantly on guard over the Vancouver Forest Region. And when that time comes, as inevitably it must, when the *Hawaii* and *Philippine Mars* take their last thundering, foaming takeoffs, let us hope that a fitting pantheon will be ready to receive and preserve them: someplace where they and the exploits of the men who flew them will be recorded ever green.

BELLA COOLA

Edith Iglauer

BELLA COOLA. The name caught my eye on a map of Canada long before I ever dreamed of moving to British Columbia. I saw BELLA COOLA at the end of one section of a jagged waterway called North Bentinck Arm, part of a fjord that made a deep cut in the coastline. The words stood out because they were, I mistakenly thought, so Spanish,

so romantic, in among a lot of Indian and Anglo-Saxon place names. I longed, for no logical reason, to go there some day.

I came to British Columbia for the first time in 1968 on a camping trip with my two young sons, Jay and Richard. We flew out from New York, where we were living, and rented a station wagon in Vancouver, camped in provincial parks and followed a route marked in heavy black ink on a worn road map that I clutched like a security blanket. Bella Coola was not one of the marked stops, but I figured we would make a side trip there if we possibly could.

Our route took us north on Vancouver Island, by ferry boat to Prince Rupert, along the Skeena River and down into the Chilcotin, to Williams Lake. At a crossroads there I saw a sign pointing west that said, BELLA COOLA.

We turned down a bumpy, dusty dirt road and stopped for gas. "How far is it to Bella Coola?" I asked.

The man selling the gas looked us up and down, stopped chewing tobacco long enough to spit accurately into a trash can and said, "How long you got?"

"Only today," I said. "I thought we'd go and take a look."

He shook his head. "It's a couple of hours just to get to the road," he said. "The Bella Coola Road. You driving?"

I said I was, and he shook his head again. "That's a pretty rough road. You better come back when you got more time. Plenty of time."

John Daly.

In 1973 I met my second husband John Daly, a commercial salmon fisherman, and went fishing with him on his forty-one-foot troller, the *Morekelp*. One season we had to stop work suddenly for a whole month because the fishermen went on strike. We were in Namu, where BC Packers has an upcoast fish-buying installation in summer, when the strike started, so we decided to go on our boat to Eucott Bay and visit two elderly gentlemen, Frenchy and Simpson, who lived there on a rotting fish-camp float. On the way in I looked at the map and saw that we were now inside the same fjord-like waterway system as Bella Coola, and said, "I wish we could go there!"

By coincidence, on our way out of Eucott we met Al Perkins, a big man with a large black moustache, who was an old friend of John's. We stopped to admire his handsome new white troller, the *Salmon Stalker*, and he remarked, "I've just been to Bella Coola, where I've been looking for land. I live in Duncan, and that place is getting too crowded for me."

"I know what you mean," John replied. "I've been thinking of doing the same thing myself."

The next morning John said, "I think we ought to explore the idea of moving to Bella Coola ourselves," as he started the boat's motor. We were soon moving along back down from where we had come, and part way he turned left, and right, into new territory; I lost track of our direction in the winding passages. The channel had high rock borders, and as we proceeded, mile after mile, twisting and turning through a steep-sided corridor, snow-capped mountains appeared ahead, above and around us. We must have gone at least fifty miles, deeper and deeper into the fjord, until we were in the narrow reach of North Bentinck Arm.

While we were running, I plucked our reference book, *British Columbia Coast Names* out from under the mattress on John's bunk and looked up Bella Coola. Spanish origin indeed! According to the book's author, Captain John Walbran, the name Bella Coola is "an adaptation of the name of a tribe of Indians residing in the neighbourhood," and Bella Coola is "the local spelling used by the postal authorities," and only one of several ways of spelling it; the others being Bela Kula; Bellaghchoolas; and Bel-houla. So much for Spain and romance!

After eight miles, we arrived at an area of mudflats and swamp grass swathed in mist. Low red buildings marked CANADIAN FISH COMPANY were on our left, and to our right were a mass of floats crowded with the boats of other commercial fishermen on strike; plus the usual mix of sailboats and pleasure cruisers. Behind this picturesque jumble were the highest mountains I had yet seen on the mountainous BC coast, with snowy tips and the white streaks of glaciers on their slopes. "It's like Switzerland here," I said. "These mountains have that same lofty beauty." I looked at the chart to reassure myself. "Bella Coola! What a surprise!" I

John and Edith.

exclaimed. "I didn't know it would be so lovely. I guess I didn't know anything about it at all."

John was busy looking for a place on the floats to tie up. He stopped beside a troller about the size of ours, the *Jan-Jac-Ann*. When our ropes were securely fastened to it, he came in and said, "Bella Coola has a big fishing fleet, and a strong union group. I've *always* thought I'd like to live in Bella Coola some day. When Al Perkins talked about moving here, I decided we'd take a look too. I don't know how much longer I can stand the noise of those airplanes flying in and out of Garden Bay, and the crowds. All the things I came to Pender Harbour to get away from are catching up with us. What I like about people in Port Hardy and the Bella Coola-ites is they don't want to increase the gross national product, they want to garden, and stay as they are. They do get tourists who fly in to hunt or fish, and a few drive in, but coming over that road is a long and hairy trip. I don't think Bella Coola is likely to get the hordes of tourists we get. At least, that's how it seems to me."

It had been raining, but now, at the end of the day, the sun took a notion to shine. I stood on our deck, dazzled by the scenery; fading rays of sun lit up the mountains, their glaciers and their valleys. "Is *this* Bella Coola?" I asked. "I don't see any houses."

"Oh, it's a two-mile walk to 'downtown' Bella Coola," John said. "I hope the telephone on the dock works. Last time I was here, the rain was *pouring* when I went up to phone you in New York, and most of the glass in the kiosk was smashed out. All I got was a recorded voice, and I lost the money I had put in, besides. I walked into Bella Coola three or four times and tried to telephone. I reported the phone the first day, and when it wasn't fixed the second night, I put my foot through the last whole piece of glass and you know why? Because I kept getting that bloody recorded voice that said, 'The number you have reached is not in service.' It just enraged me. If I had a human answer I would have been far less mad. Those fiendish recorded voices are an atrocity against all who cannot afford phones in their own houses; a non-humanity that causes real angry frustration. I certainly understand the violent vandalism that occurs in an inarticulate 'won't answer back' phone booth." With that, he turned and marched up the ramp to telephone.

The telephone must have worked, because he was back shortly to say we had been invited for supper by the local game warden, Tony Karup. He arrived shortly in a yellow government truck; a greying, bald man in a khaki uniform. He drove us along a road bordered by the grassy flats of a river

25

estuary that appeared to be a dumping ground for dilapidated and abandoned boats; and then we were in the main part of the town of Bella Coola. It consisted of a few rectangular streets, a United Church hospital, a library, several churches and stores. He pointed out a large store, famous for its excellent stock of books and handicrafts, that was owned and run by a local author, Cliff Kopas, whose book, *Bella Coola*, has become a standard historical reference. Driving along, it was clear that most of the Indian population in town lived on one side of the main intersection and the white people on the other.

We spent a pleasant evening at the neat, official house of the game warden and his good-looking Danish wife, but our meal was interrupted several times by telephoned reports about a grizzly bear in the area. "It's been killing cattle right in town, and I don't want any vigilante action," Tony said, returning to the table looking worried. "Everybody's complaining now about all kinds of bears since they heard about this one; about bears that show up at their back doors, or claw marks on the windows, or garbage bags ripped apart. I was talking to one of our best Indian guides this morning, and he said, 'If I want to attract a bear for my clients, I buy new bread and they can smell it for miles around.' He also told me, 'I was at the garbage dump yesterday and I felt the wind of a paw on the back of my neck, and I sure jumped into the cab of my truck in a hurry!'"

The next morning, John and I walked the two miles into town in drizzling rain that shortly turned into a downpour. While we were wandering around in the Cliff Kopas store a tall, cheerful man greeted John. He was walking with the aid of two canes, and his name was Tom Gee. The last time John had seen him he was gillnetting. John called to me several counters away and I arrived in time to hear that Gee had jumped off a roof and landed on his heels, breaking them both.

Tom hustled us into his truck and for the several more days we stayed in Bella Coola he was our guide and transportation. That was fortunate because it never stopped raining. The rain in Bella Coola had a special wetness that gave everything a damp aura, and even soaked through my fairly waterproof red windbreaker. Even now, when I am asked my impression of Bella Coola, all I can remember is the rain—and the friendliness of the people.

One morning when Tom arrived to pick us up he said, "I thought we'd go up the Bella Coola Road, oh, just for an hour or so." He explained as we drove away that the local inhabitants had built the road themselves. It was a tremendous effort, over the mountain range that separated Bella Coola by land from any other community. It connected over the top of the range to the town of Anahim Lake, where my sons and I would have landed if we had been foolish enough to keep on driving from Williams Lake.

John said, "I've never been on that road. It's the only land route in and out of Bella Coola. The only other way to go is by boat or plane, and often the weather's so bad planes can't fly. The government wouldn't do anything about a road, so the Bella Coola people built their own. I think they got a little grant for dynamite. Constructing that road over that mountain range was an extraordinary achievement."

"What's the road like?" I asked.

John replied, "I once met the man in charge of roads for the government and he said to me, 'It's really embarrassing. When I make road inspections my wife and daughter sometimes come with me, but when I start down the Bella Coola Road, they either insist on staying at Anahim or they drive in with me with a rug over their heads.'"

We turned and started up a gravel road through a valley. Tom stopped once to show us an old water wheel, and again to let cattle cross in front of us. We drove past Indian smokehouses, sheds with rows of deep red salmon hanging on lines, then a federal fisheries counting hut that looked like an outhouse perched over a stream, and then a house shaped like an ark. "Here's hippyville in Noah's Ark," Tom said, and then we were crossing a bridge over rushing water. "A truck went through here when the bridge collapsed, and a little boy drowned," he said. "The fellow driving found the boy pinned under a bunker." We passed a handsome farm. "That belongs to the biggest farmer around here; he also has a house in town," Tom said.

Somewhere along the way, near where Tom said the Bella Coola River joined with the white water of another river, I saw a sign that said, 'Closed to bear hunting. Do not feed, tease or molest bears.' The road was becoming steeper and below us was spread a vista of beautiful bare green hills and snow slides. Tom was driving in first gear now, very, very slowly. Rocks slid down, rolling around the fenders of the truck.

I saw Tom put his elbows on the wheel, steering with them while he lit a cigarette. It was a horrifying sight. "You'd be surprised at the number of people who come in and don't drive out again," he said casually. "They put their cars on a barge instead and fly home. The road was just a goat trail when I came over it in 1956, and pretty tough here in the beginning; not the way it is now, with lots of turnbacks and turnarounds. Hello there!" he exclaimed, as a boulder hit the truck and rolled over the embankment.

I was sitting between the two men, so I had to stretch my neck to see where the rock had gone. The boulder bounced along until it disappeared into what looked to me like a bottomless chasm, at least two thousand feet down.

We stopped suddenly. A large truck was just ahead, which shocked me. We could see such a short distance in front of us that I thought we had the road to ourselves. We sat and waited while the truck backed up over the edge. Its rear end hung out over space while it made the sharp turn in the road to go forward again.

Gee said, "Someone asked a trucker friend of mine how he did this in winter, when it's a sheet of ice and he said, 'Nothin' to it. I just drink a gallon of goof at the top of the hill and it smooths out like a prairie.'"

There was a general chuckle, which I joined in weakly. Then we went through the same manoeuvre we had watched the truck make; backing over the edge in a switchback, to go forward. I tried not to think about the back end of our truck hanging out into space while we sat in the front end.

"There's never been a fatal accident on this road," Tom continued cheerfully. "A fellow went over in a Toyota station wagon with a load of sewing machines 'way up past here, and dropped sixty feet onto a switchback below, hit a tree and hung up there. It wrecked the tree, and he was in the hospital for two or three days. That's all. People drive this road at a crawl because they know they have to, even if they are drunk."

We were grinding our way up the road again, catching up to the truck ahead of us, then falling back to wait. We continued to stop and back up at each hairpin turn on what I now viewed as an insane road, admirable as the effort must have been to build it. I was not put at ease by Gee's steering with his elbows again as he lit another cigarette. John was silent, but I must have stirred nervously in my seat between them, because to ease the tension Gee said, "There were four bears on Main Street last night. One about four hundred pounds was seen in the telephone booth, probably phoning to find out where the garbage dump is, and when he came out someone saw him pick up a garbage can and walk off with it. A bear scattered a garbage pail on the back porch of the hotel, and another bear was seen by the beer hall, looking in store windows. I guess they're taking the path of least resistance and not picking berries any more. Tony finally shot one last night."

I was beyond conversation; just hoping, well, praying, that Tom wouldn't light another cigarette. When I thought I couldn't stand looking over one more thousand or two thousand or whatever thousand-

The stern of the Morekelp.

27

foot drop on another hairpin switchback turn, I saw a turnaround ahead. John glanced at his watch and cleared his throat. Tom said, "Do you think we'd better go back now? We're having supper with the matron of the hospital, who wants to meet you, and we shouldn't be late."

"I think we'd better," John said. We turned around and headed back. My relief was short-lived. Going down was worse. Looking through the windshield, the short span of road ahead extended only a few feet and disappeared in the vertical drop. Then, over the edge and down we went, to another vanishing point and another steep drop, prefaced by a switchback that left us teetering over the side of the mountain. I tried looking ahead. Glancing over the side, across John, was not a pleasing view either — just emptiness, nothing below as far as I could see from where I sat, except on the switchbacks, where I could unfortunately see exactly how far down it was into the canyons beneath us. I thought about the mother and daughter who drove with a blanket over their heads. I wished I had brought one with me. I would have used it, without shame.

John put his hand over mine. He said, "Tom, I heard you had some sort of an accident with your gillnetter. What happened?"

"I was off Egg Island, and the engine started to miss," Tom said, throwing his cigarette out the window. I took a stick of gum out of my purse and started chewing, bracing myself for the moment when he would light another cigarette. Mercifully, he didn't. "As soon as I turned off the switch she blew, and blew me right out over the drum into the water," he continued. "I think the fire caught in the fuel pump. I didn't have a skiff along, so I swam away from the boat and got mixed up in some kelp. Then I swam back to the boat, got a grip on the tail end of the net, and made a hand hold. With the stablizer and poles and the mast coming down, I felt

pretty small, I can tell you. Everything burning and no skiff; and a hundred and twenty dollars in my pocket that I couldn't use. I was sure I'd be picked up because I had seen the Air Rescue on Egg Island. Somebody finally *did* pick me up, but I've always taken a skiff with me since then. I don't know when I'll get back fishing though. Breaking all those little bones in your heels is *really* painful, and they take a long time to heal."

We were down in the woods, in the valley now, driving through lovely green forests. I sat back with an audible sigh of relief. "If we had gone the whole way to Anahim, how long is that road?" I asked.

"Two hundred and fifty miles," Tom said.

"And that's the *only* way out of Bella Coola by land?" I asked.

"That's right," John said.

Back on the boat that night I said to John, "If you move to Bella Coola, I'll come and visit you. Maybe." He laughed and turned on the news. A few minutes later, the fisherman on the *Jan-Jac-Ann* told us that a strike vote had been called for the next day in Namu.

It was time to leave anyway. The continual rasp of our boat rocking against its neighbour, the rumble of the Gardner motor being run to prevent the chilly damp from overwhelming us, particularly in my quarters below, and the endless patter of raindrops on the pilothouse roof were getting on our nerves. For the first and only time on the *Morekelp*, we began to snap at one another.

I packed for travelling; stowing loose items in the sink, ramming a knife in the cupboard door to keep it shut. The sun came out, casting a lovely yellow-white light on the mountains as we moved slowly away from the dock. I had seen Bella Coola, at last. It was beautiful, just as I had imagined, but I had no regrets about leaving.

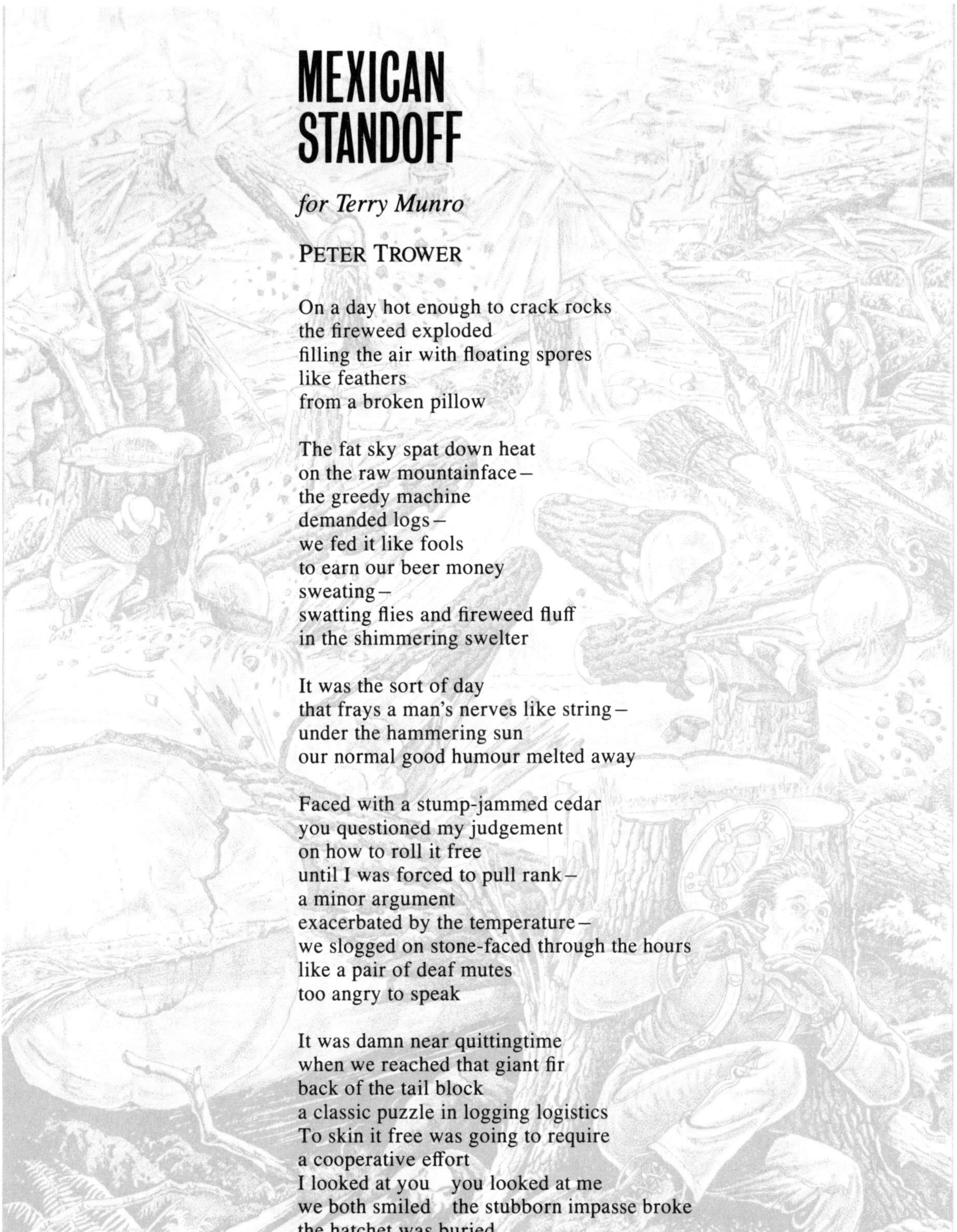

MEXICAN STANDOFF

for Terry Munro

PETER TROWER

On a day hot enough to crack rocks
the fireweed exploded
filling the air with floating spores
like feathers
from a broken pillow

The fat sky spat down heat
on the raw mountainface—
the greedy machine
demanded logs—
we fed it like fools
to earn our beer money
sweating—
swatting flies and fireweed fluff
in the shimmering swelter

It was the sort of day
that frays a man's nerves like string—
under the hammering sun
our normal good humour melted away

Faced with a stump-jammed cedar
you questioned my judgement
on how to roll it free
until I was forced to pull rank—
a minor argument
exacerbated by the temperature—
we slogged on stone-faced through the hours
like a pair of deaf mutes
too angry to speak

It was damn near quittingtime
when we reached that giant fir
back of the tail block
a classic puzzle in logging logistics
To skin it free was going to require
a cooperative effort
I looked at you   you looked at me
we both smiled   the stubborn impasse broke
the hatchet was buried
We set to work
parbuckled the big blue butt out of there
and became friends again.

the Worst Storm in Sunshine Coast History

HELEN DAWE

IN THE FAMOUS GREAT GALE of Saturday, January 21, 1921, heavy timber along the coast went down before a southeast wind, making a shambles of several communities. Pioneers living at early coastal settlements published accounts and told stories to younger generations.

In Great Waters, a book written by the Reverend George Pringle, includes an account of the storm at Lang Bay, which lies on the east side of Malaspina Strait, south of Powell River. Pringle and five others from a shinglebolt camp were walking the mile through the woods to Smith's store at the Lang Bay settlement when the 1921 gale "tore down upon us in howling fury. There was no place for shelter from the great branches and limbs that whizzed past us in the darkness, and the giant trees that fell crashing down in all directions around us. The noise of the storm was so great that to make ourselves heard we had to shout into one another's ears."

The marine missionary wrote that he spent the most terrifying hour of his life on that walk, but upon arriving at a house at Smith's clearing he decided to hold his service anyway: "We were nicely started when the window blew in! I caught it on my back, but the lamp was extinguished and the table blown over. It took fifteen minutes to get the window nailed back and everything in order again. I got along to the sermon and was somewhere in 'secondly' when a wild blast commenced to tear the paper off the wall opposite me, against which the people were sitting. It was building paper loosely tacked on in strips from ceiling to floor. Another gust and down it all came, completely covering up my congregation. After they had crawled out it took half an hour before we got that paper tacked up again. Then we closed with the hymn 'For Those in Peril on the Sea.' Millions of feet of standing timber were blown down that night at Lang Bay."

Mr. and Mrs. William Griffith and their youngsters settled in August, 1920 at a bay east of Egmont Point, which is northeast of Skookumchuk Narrows. They lived in a log cabin which had been built by a relative in 1914. When Mrs. Griffith proposed putting the children to bed on that Saturday evening in January, 1921, Mr. Griffith suggested a delay because a southeast wind was refreshing. Gladys McNutt recorded their story as told to her by the Griffiths' son Bill.

"The Griffiths wrapped up the children and took them out to a bare rocky islet within the bay and spread canvas over them as protection from the flying twigs and needles."

Early Sunday morning a few of the men who lived in the Egmont area rowed over to check on the Griffith household.

"They breathed a sigh of relief to see smoke coming from the chimney but a huge limb was through the roof immediately above the spot where Mr. Griffith usually sat. They all got busy and felled the maples and alders about the place. Most of the standing timber in the draw had come down."

Florence E. Montgomery and Alice French told me how the gale had affected them half a century before. Mrs. Montgomery was at that time Florence Cliff, the first teacher at the original West Sechelt School. She boarded for a time with Katie Deal and her husband Fred near the Trail Bay beach. On the Saturday afternoon of the big storm, Florence took a bath and dressed in her best for a dance at the Selma Park Pavilion. She was all ready when Mr. Deal arrived home. He told the ladies to put out the lamps and douse the fire to avoid trouble should a tree fall on the house. Then he shepherded his wife, Florence, as well as the neighbours, Mrs. Nickson and her children Rena and Harold, to take shelter on the beach in the lee of a large scow stranded there two or three years earlier.

About one o'clock Sunday morning the wind had abated sufficiently that Fred Deal felt it safe for his charges to return home. A tree had fallen near the Deal house, but both residences in Nickson's Bay were safe. When daylight came they walked up Norwest Bay Road to West Sechelt School and, en route, counted twenty-four trees down.

Alice French came to Sechelt in 1919 as the English war bride of Frank French. She was a friend of Thomas John Cook who, as resident magistrate, knew everybody for miles about and organized his neighbours to check on the more isolated homesteads on the day after the storm. He assigned Alice to visit Mr. and Mrs. McIntyre in West Sechelt. She found them flourishing and their home intact, but their outdoor privy had vanished completely. During the next summer Alice attended a tea party in the McIntyres' garden. She happened to look up into a tree shading her chair and to her amusement saw the can from the lost outhouse perched high on a limb.

It is said that the giant trees and snags which fell before the southeaster usually lay pointing to the northwest, sometimes piled two or three deep. For years, the trees brought down by the gale provided firewood for the homesteaders. What a vast amount of time and energy it must have cost to get the trunks sawn through before power saws were in use, to clear the primitive roads, and to restore downed telegraph wires. Electric lighting did not then exist except for households using private systems. The West Sechelt School in 1921 had only candles and the Sechelt store used hanging gas lamps, which gave a nice white light.

From *Helen Dawe's Sechelt* by Helen Dawe, Harbour Publishing, 1990.

The Sechelt Wharf undergoing repairs, likely following the 1921 storm.

FIRE·*UP ABOVE*

FIRE·*DOWN BELOW*

LILLIAN LAMONT BATEMAN

THE SPRING AND SUMMER OF 1922 brought unusually hot and dry weather to the Horseshoe Valley. Mother's small garden struggled and died in spite of the water we carried from the creek. The trees had become crisp and dry, and even the toughest bushes were losing their leaves. This was prime forest fire weather, yet none of the logging operations had shut down, because in 1922 there were no regulations. The logging companies, including Brooks Scanlon O'Brien in the Horseshoe Valley, were left to stop work in the woods at their own discretion, and so long as there was a dollar to be made they kept on cutting.

August arrived hotter and drier than ever. Each morning mother went out to search the sky, hoping to see clouds that would bring us the relief of rain.

The creek was already low, and threatening to dry up. If that happened we had no other source of water, since our well was always dry.

Forest fires had already broken out on the coast. That was where dad was now, fighting a fire that threatened Stillwater. It had already destroyed a logging outfit near Myrtle Point and was now burning near Lang Bay. Before it was over hundreds of acres of prime timber were burned, the logging equipment was destroyed and the company was rendered bankrupt.

Fire fighting in the early twenties was simply men against the flames. They had no chain saws, bulldozers or water bombers, no fire retardant to drop from the air. Men only had shovels, axes, crosscut saws and "back-firing." There was no two-

Stillwater in May 1923.

The house in the Horseshoe Valley that we left in 1922.

way radio then. It was dangerous work. Trapped between fires, men burned to death. Others were struck by falling trees or cut with axes, or they collapsed from sheer exhaustion.

Why did they volunteer? It paid well, and most men, like dad, were glad to get the work. It's been said some settlers actually set fires in order to earn a "grub stake" for the winter. Dad certainly hadn't started this fire, but he was reaping the benefits from it and had promised Mama to be careful. That didn't stop her worrying though, because he'd not been in touch with us for a week.

One August afternoon at about four o'clock Mama handed me a pail. I knew what that meant—I'd forgotten to bring her the usual bucket of fresh water before she started supper. At the train tracks I paused as usual to be sure no engine or speeder was on the line. The track was clear, but something strange was happening in the sky north of us where the rails disappeared into the trees.

Big creamy-pink clouds were climbing up the sky. They reminded me of clouds reflecting the setting sun, only I knew the sun didn't set in the north. Could they be thunderclouds? I'd never seen any like this before.

Returning with the water, I reported the "funny" clouds to mother. Alarmed, she dropped the paring knife and was out the door like a shot. Mother guessed before even reaching the track that my "clouds" had to be smoke. She'd seen too many fires

when she lived in Montana not to know smoke clouds, and one look convinced her we were in trouble.

Over a very hasty supper, Mother made plans to defend our home. First we'd fill every pot, pan, pail, tub and wash-boiler with water and try to finish the job before dark. We'd collect blankets and be ready to soak them in Dad's old tub. If the fire came in our direction a wet blanket would protect us long enough to reach the creek. If worse came to worst we'd go lie down in the water.

Right now the fire seemed to be somewhere north of Camp Three, but the wind can shift and hot ash travels several miles, so Mother figured we'd better be prepared to wet down the roof. She put a ladder against the house and said I'd have to pass pails of water up for her to throw on the roof.

I listened but couldn't take it all in. It seemed a nightmare, a bad dream. I kept expecting to wake up. Meanwhile, we'd been hauling water until we'd filled everything in the house. The sun had gone down behind the western mountains but north of us the sky was a dark and angry red.

By bedtime the sky glowed beyond the fringe of the forest. The trees where the twin rails converged stood out in silhouette against the burning sky. The night wind was quite hot, and I thought I could smell smoke though the wind blew from the south. Was there another fire below us? Suddenly I shivered.

I doubt that Mother slept very much that night but I was asleep as soon as my head hit the pillow. How

Mother, myself and Sammy in 1922.

I wished Daddy were home to tell us what to do! If I remembered to say my prayers that night you can be sure I really meant them.

At six a.m. sharp I was wakened by the shrill whistle of the train. It was so loud, so close, that for a second or two I was sure I'd been dreaming. Then I heard the release of steam, and jumping out of bed I ran to the window just as Dad dropped from the cab and the train moved off. I made a dash for the stairs but by the time I got to the front door Mama had beat me to it. She stood there hugging him and saying things like "thank God you're here" and how scared she'd been all night, until he pushed her away saying he had no time to talk now, we had until eleven o'clock to get everything packed and be ready to get out. All the settlers in the valley were being evacuated. We'd be going to a camp they'd set up in Stillwater. This fire at Camp Three was the worst yet. Some damn fool had been running a donkey and sparks from its smokestack had set fire to a pile of slash. The way the fire was heading it looked like it would sweep the whole damn valley.

I don't recall eating breakfast but I do remember packing my dolls. I also put all my precious doll dishes in a small wooden box and stowed it under the bank in the creek. Mama allowed me to keep Teddy but my best doll, Effie, and all the other toys went in the big trunk Dad was going to put down the well. He'd been lowering stuff into the dry well ever since he got home. Mama's cabinet sewing machine, her two trunks, boxes of dishes and boxes of books.

By the time two trunks and half a dozen boxes were lowered into the sixteen-foot dry well it was full and ready to be covered with a tarp and a foot of dirt. Mama couldn't even hide the big family Bible. She asked Dad to dig another hole but he cussed, saying it could stay in the house and burn for all he cared. So what if it was a family heirloom? Then Mama found a place to hide it in case the house didn't burn. She put it over the front door, jammed in between the two-by-fours. She told Dad where she put it and said it would protect the house. That made Dad cuss some more and tell her she was a damn fool and it was such goddamn superstition that was wrong with the world.

But Mama's faith in the Holy Book proved to be well placed. Whether there was anything in her idea or not, our house did not burn, though the fire raged in the woods all around us. Not so much as a shingle got scorched, not that it mattered. Mother never entered or saw that house again.

By eleven a.m. we were ready to leave. Everything was in the well save the kitchen range, a few pots and pans, the heater and the beds. Dad had his precious bagpipes, violin and tool box ready to go, Mother had two suitcases and a large purse packed with medical supplies, things we'd need in an emergency. Dad's jacket pockets bulged with sandwiches and cookies. There'd be something to eat if we got stuck on the road. At this point we'd no idea where our next meal was coming from or whether we'd reach Stillwater at all.

Right on schedule, at eleven a.m., the Big Baldwin with our two friends Boris and Steve paused in front of the house. They had a single boxcar in tow, the reason they'd made the run in the first place. Our dog Laddie, the suitcases and Dad's stuff were put in the boxcar. We'd been invited to ride up in the cab with the crew.

It was a ride I'll never forget. To actually stand beside Boris and see all those mysterious gauges and levers while the rails were disappearing under us was like living a dream. What surprised me most was the heat and how much coal Steve had to shovel into the fire box so uncomfortably close to my rear.

Then abruptly Boris slowed, braked, stopped the Baldwin, leaned out the cab window and spoke to someone holding a red flag beside the track. Turning to Dad, he said, "Sorry, Sam, but this is as far as we go. The fire's run up the Copenhagen Canyon. The big trestle's timbers are burning in a few places, and they can't tell how much damage has been done. I can't risk taking the engine across so you will all have to get off here. There's a speeder waiting down the track a ways, near Hand's old road. He'll run you down to the coast."

We all thanked Boris and Steve. Dad helped us down from the engine then went to collect the dog and whatever we had in the baggage car. Loaded down with luggage and boxes, we started off down the track to find the speeder.

The man running the speeder was one of the company's brakemen. Either Hannigan or Hank Morell. He helped Dad load the speeder and told us where to sit. Dad, Mother, my little bother Sammy and Laddie were on the front. The bags were piled wherever they could make room. I sat at the rear beside a strange man who looked as if he ate kids.

The driver handed out smelly wet blankets and told us to keep them over our shoulders and be ready to duck under them when "things got too hot." Mama dug into her handbag for the carbolated Vaseline, saying it might prevent blisters if the air got too hot. Being the obedient one, I applied it to my face without argument but Sammy kicked up one helluva row and by the time Mama finished with him she had more of it on her than he had on his face. Then with a few more instructions our driver said, "Hang on!" and we were off.

Speeders are noisy, and this one's engine echoing off the walls of the canyon made it even noisier. Still, the driver managed to shout over the din to tell us, "There's a hot spot not far ahead. If it's too bad I'll have to stop and wait till the wind drops, then make a run for it. Can't take a chance on getting caught when the fire jumps the track! You guys keep down! Stay under the blankets." Then only a few seconds after the warning the speeder suddenly stopped.

I knew we were pretty close to the trestle when a sharp curve flung me against my neighbour. A moment later Hank slammed on the brakes. I remember bumping my head. The noisy engine was almost quiet, just single pop-pops now so it let in all the other sounds. They flooded over me like a cataract.

We remained still for what seemed hours. Under the stinky old blanket I got hot, nervous, felt I couldn't breathe. So I threw off the blanket in panic. What I saw will be with me to my grave, it's burned into my mind forever, like a vision of Hell.

To the left the once well-forested mountain is now a mass of charred logs, broken and still smouldering. Countless corpses of great trees have been thrown down in confusion. Occasionally seal flames rise and dance for a moment, smoke eddies up, twists and writhes like pale ghosts. A few trees are still standing, bare of branches, while flames lick their way around them as if eating them alive.

Fascinated, I watched such a tree not more than one hundred feet ahead. Suddenly, with a tremendous roaring noise, it flung a single sheet of orange flame across the track like a blast from a blowtorch. Its target—one single surviving fir on the opposite bank. The victim exploded with a crack like a shot. Nothing was left but a few blackened limbs and the trunk.

It happened in the blink of an eye. One minute there was a young fir tree, now there was nothing but a smoking skeleton. I also noticed something else. Some of the ties under the track ahead of us were on fire, burning with short blue flames, reminding me of brandy blazing on a Christmas pudding. Later I heard it was the oil that had dripped from the trains that caused the ties to burn blue.

After that extraordinary flame bursting over the tracks the fire seemed to pause, its roar subsided, the wind dropped. That gave Hank time to make his run for it, taking me by surprise.

I'd not had time to duck under the blanket. When the speeder took off, I had all I could do to stay on the seat. I was still hanging on for dear life when something struck me in my left eye. The pain was excruciating. I'm sure I screamed but in all the racket no one heard or paid any attention, which was just as well. There was nothing they could do about it anyway. I curled up in misery and cried into the dirty, smelly blanket until we stopped and got off the speeder just above the camp. I suppose the tears were helpful, nature's way of cooling the injured tissue and washing away the dirt.

Mother and the driver were quite concerned when they inspected my burned eye but Dad wasn't. He swore and said if I'd kept my head under the damned blanket as I'd been told to do in the first place this wouldn't have happened. I was a bloody nuisance and No, he didn't think I should go to the first aid shack. He didn't want that quack playing doctor with one of his kids.

Mama surprised me (and Dad, no doubt) by overruling his edict. She said she was going to have my eye "looked to" and asked the driver where the first aid was. We found the first aid man set up in a corner of one of the offices. He sat me down and after a bit of fuss on my part, examined the eye. I had a burn all right, but not where it would interfere with my sight. He'd flush it and put some medication in and a bandage over it so I'd not rub or irritate it further.

How conspicuous and foolish I felt with that white gauze on my head! Wherever we went people stopped Mama to ask what had happened to the little girl's eye. It embarrassed us both and didn't make Mama any easier to live with. She deplored being the centre of attention. It smacked of ill-breeding. The way she acted you'd think I'd burned my eye on purpose, just to have strangers stop and ask questions. I spent a miserable afternoon and evening and was delighted to get rid of the bandage the next day.

Dad, Sammy, our dog Laddie and I in Stillwater in 1923.

Hotel, Stillwater, 1925.

Union Steamship Lady Cecilia *arriving at Stillwater.*

But the day wasn't a total loss. That evening the refugees — and there must have been forty or fifty of us — went to the camp cookhouse to eat. Some had been here in camp several days already, people from the Lang Bay/Myrtle Point fire area as well as the ones from the Horseshoe Valley. Many appeared foreign. Dressed in strange clothes, they spoke languages I couldn't understand, but they all knew what to do with the ice cream. Yes! Ice cream! The first I'd had since leaving Vancouver almost two years ago!

It seems the company had ordered several commercial cartons of strawberry ice cream (at least that's how I remember it), and for the first time in my life, I actually had more ice cream than I could eat. It had arrived on the evening boat just in time for our very first meal as refugees and put everyone in good humour, a clever move on the part of Brooks Scanlon O'Brien, since it was their greed and carelessness that had driven us out in the first place. Dad figured that out later, but I remember him eating his share of the ice cream first.

The ice cream was one thing, falling asleep in a bunkhouse filled with noisy strangers was another. Mother, Sammy and I shared one narrow bunk, with me at the foot. Try to fall asleep in that position with a sore eye and babies howling, women snoring and others recounting their life stories! Some kept up a running commentary on the camp, the food, their personal loss and the present state of their health. Others cried. What would they return to? Everything would be in ashes. All they had left in this world were the clothes they stood up in. Not all spoke English, some sounded like German or Slav.

We'd not completely undressed that night, only removed our skirts, blouses and shoes. Mother had taken the precaution of hiding our shoes under the blanket at the top of the bed. She didn't trust foreigners and to find herself surrounded by them was very nerve-wracking indeed. She also lay with her purse under her pillow, its strap over her wrist. I say "lay" because I doubt Mother closed an eye all night.

The latrines were outside, very primitive and not very sanitary, even by 1920s standards. We washed in tin basins out on a bench, tossing the dirty water over the swamp behind the bunkhouses. The refugees' dogs were tied out behind the cookhouse, staked far enough apart to keep them from fighting. Fed scraps from the cookhouse, they'd never had it so good.

Once we were dressed, washed and reasonably tidy, Mama set out for the cookhouse. Dad had promised to meet us there and Mama was "dying" for her morning cup of tea. Naturally when we got there he hadn't arrived, so instead of standing around waiting we went in and found a place fairly close to the door at one of the long tables. Mama got her tea, Sammy and I some milk and we sat facing the door waiting to catch sight of Daddy.

We didn't have long to wait. Dad appeared shortly and was remarkably bright and cheerful. Mama asked if he'd had a good night's sleep. He had, but that wasn't the good news, and as soon as he got himself another cup of coffee he'd tell us all about what he'd just found out.

Dad said he'd got up early, had breakfast and was out for a walk, just taking a look around, when he ran into a guy he'd met one time coming up on the boat. They got to talking and it turns out this guy is one of the old timers, guy by the name of McRae.

"He's got a farm down the coast a bit and when I told him the fix we're in, looking for a place to stay, he said there was an old shack in his bay we could batch in for the time being. I said we'd take it.

The old floathouse dad fixed up for us to live in, 1923.

Whatever it is, it'll be a helluva lot better than hanging around here."

Mama agreed but she had a lot of questions, few of which Dad could answer, though he did know how to get there because McRae had told him the farm was two and a half miles to the south at the end of an old skid road. McRae told Dad he'd come out from Ontario twenty-odd years ago, had taken out a preemption on a large piece of BC's coast and logged it before settling down to farm.

He was married, had two sons by a mail-order bride, had a fine home. The shack we'd use was one his hired hand batched in during the harvest. This information relieved Mother. At least she'd have a woman to talk to. Anything would be better than hanging around the refugee camp waiting for news about the fire and worrying about our house.

This was the first good news we'd heard so far and in almost no time we'd collected our belongings and were ready to leave for McRae's. The only delay was when Mama insisted we buy a few provisions, so Dad got them at the company store: tea, coffee, sugar, flour, baking powder, salt and rolled oats, though Dad told her we could borrow from McRae for a day or so while we got settled. We all started out with a load, except Sammy of course...and the least said about how he'd been behaving the better.

As soon as we were ready to leave, Dad collected Laddie, making our family complete, and we started down the road for McRae's cove.

In retrospect, I'd say the forest fire that chased us off the Horseshoe Valley homestead was a stroke of good luck. We ended up settling by the ocean, and I was able to attend school regularly for the first time. Leaving the Horseshoe Valley must have been a great disappointment to my parents though, especially for Dad, since he'd made nearly every board that went into it and built the house alone with his own two hands.

After staying a while at McRae's shack, we bought a float house on Maude Bay. It took time to get all the necessary work done on the house and it was February of 1923 — five months after the fire — before Dad got up to the old homestead to get the rest of the boxes he'd stored in the well. When he got there, he found that the same well that had always been dry held four feet of water and almost everything, including Mom's trunk and her sewing machine, was soaked. Many of our books were ruined, and Mama's fine table linens were stained permanently. It seems ironic that while the house had been spared, many of the items stowed in the supposedly safe well were wrecked — not by fire but by water.

TWENTY MILES TO PARADISE

GOWER POINT
1917–1925

JOHN WATSON

A T TEN O'CLOCK on the morning of July 1, 1917, the small Union Steamship Company steamer let out one short warning blast from its steam whistle mounted on the forward side of the red and black funnel. The funnel was tipped with black to hide the smoke stains from the coal-burning boilers.

An experienced eye could tell by the smooth curved lines of the hull, the graceful dip and rise of the sheer line, and the rake of the funnel and the two masts that she was designed for the wind and the open sea. The curved bow line similar to the fast clipper sailing ships ended at the deck with a truncated bowsprit, the sole remains of a sailing past. Her name was SS *Chilco*, and she was 151 feet long and 305 gross tons. On another day the escape vessel might be the SS *Chasina*, a sister ship, 142 feet long and 258 gross tons. To small boys they were magnificent ships with a mysterious past.

Eventually everyone was aboard, clutching their boxes, bags, strapped-up suitcases and trunks, and trying to keep their excited galloping children from falling overboard. Among the passengers was my family, departing to spend the first of nine summers in our newly built cottage on Gower Point, near Gibsons. The vessel proceeded astern, away from the wretched tar-smelling dock, foul harbour water, and smoke-filled city.

The Vancouver we left behind was one of gravelled roads, wood plank sidewalks and horse-drawn delivery wagons, with their unique form of pollution that got buried or hidden below the planks of some wooden roads. Steam-driven, coal-fired road rollers and fire engines, and plenty of coal and wood smoke from every chimney in every house and every commercial or factory building didn't do much for clean air. There were dozens of sawmills burning wood waste in large beehive baskets fifty to one hundred feet high. The electric railway or streetcar system, with double tracks down the centres of the main streets which suddenly darted off into the bush, provided most of the city transport and links to outlying areas. This system ran on hydro-electric power, which was clean, but the same company also produced domestic cooking gas by coking or distilling coal. The city was far dirtier and smellier than it was decades later when it was ten times as big.

Photographs of street and beach scenes in this period show nearly everyone wearing black or dark-coloured clothing, even in summer. Was this because black didn't show the dirt? There were a few automobiles for the wealthy and for some delivery vans. All vehicles were black, except the red fire engines and the green streetcars. The horses were black or brown, with white ones reserved for the fire engines. Boots were black, as were stockings and bathing costumes—an apt name because they looked like they belonged on stage. During the great war of 1914–1918 the big EXTRA EXTRA headlines were thickly black, reflecting the news and the terrible

The SS Selma, *later the Union Steamship* Chasina, *in 1913 or 1914.*

losses. My brother Bradley and I were to remember always the huge coal bin in the basement, full of big lumps of soft coal and black coal dust that seemed to cover everything. All of this may have been why many families, including mine, shipped out for two months every summer to breathe the fresh clean air of the country.

The trip from Vancouver to Gower Point took about two hours – a mere fraction of the journey for those going farther up the coast. At the more populous centres, a wharf made disembarking simple, but at the unsheltered Point the best method available was a large raft or float, anchored two or three hundred yards off shore. The float was no more than forty feet square, and in rough weather it leaped up and down and around in wind and wave.

It was not easy for the Union boats to pull in close to the shore and make fast with heavy lines to the moving float. If the vessel was travelling fast enough to steer properly and made a good connection quickly, the float could be pulled by the ship, and the anchor chains could be tightened until they broke or one of the cleats on the float was pulled out. If that didn't happen, the vessel and the float rose and fell with the waves like two elevators doing a dance. This made the transfer of people somewhat risky but always fun for the kids. The passengers remaining on the boat for a safe steady wharf farther up the coast always thought the people who lived at the Point were stupid idiots, sort of Potty Pointers.

There were two other landing possibilities. When it was too rough for the float landing, the steamer whistled and Harry Chaster would row his big lap strake or clinker boat to meet the ship farther out from shore. When the ship slowed down Harry would manoeuvre his small boat up to the heaving sides and throw a line to one of the deckhands on the freight deck. This might be several feet above the water. In the brief moment when the two boats were on the same level, the passengers would leap into the rowboat like bees to a flower and have their baggage thrown after them. I don't recall anyone ever falling over the side or plunging through the bottom of Harry's boat, but there were many close calls. Occasionally, when the sea was too rough to make a safe transfer or someone got cold feet, passengers would stay on board and be carried on to the next stop. How they got back I don't know.

Hitting the beach is exactly the right way to describe how Harry's boat, and everyone else's, made first contact with the barnacle-covered rocks at low tide and the smooth round boulders at mid or high tide. With four-foot waves chasing you in, it was tricky to catch the right wave and keep the boat headed straight for the beach without tipping everyone into the cold briny water. On one occasion a bunch of boys were attempting such a landing when a wave caught the boat under the stern and flipped it up and over in the air, in a tangle of arms and legs and oars. After it came down it was a few minutes

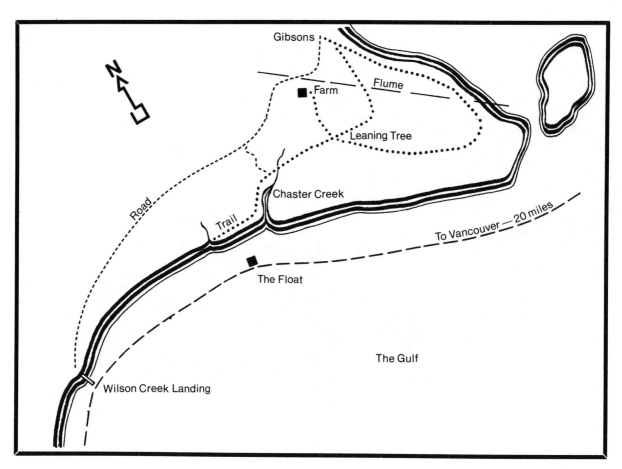

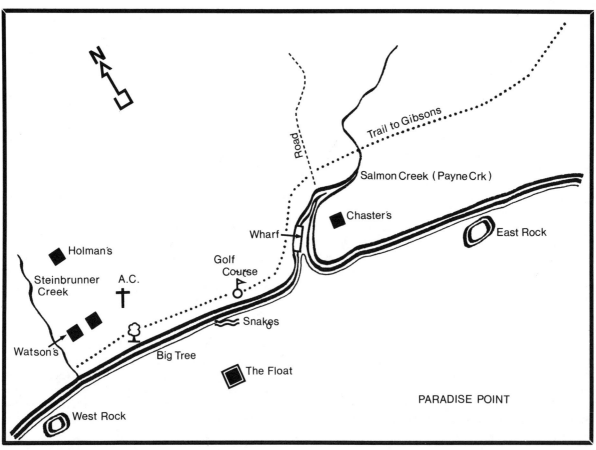

before it was noticed that one boy was missing. With the help of some onlookers the boat was pulled free of the air suction that held it down and a frightened little boy waded ashore, his face whiter than the bubbly surf.

At high tide an alternative landing place existed in a small estuary that led up into a meandering creek. The salmon found this entry easier than we did. Someone had built a small, crude landing wharf that floated up and down with the tide and was held in place by a few creosoted piles. Even here there was minimal protection from the surf, and it was almost as difficult to get in as the passage led directly onto the beach.

Our first vacation at Gower Point was in 1918, when we went for two or three weeks. My brother Bradley was eight, I was six and my sister Margaret was three. There wasn't much to do because we rented a shack near Chaster Creek and suffered from the problems of adapting to a crude and cramped living space and a rather wet summer. Containers to catch the raindrops coming through the roof were at a premium. Even the walls were inadequate, so a sign was put up which read "Look-Out-Inn." You could see both ways through the gaps in the walls and through these openings the wind whistled and the mice scampered.

This first adventure away from the city convinced Father that if he was to return to the Point another year he would have to build a house of his own, and he set out to buy some building materials for a sturdy new house. He purchased a pre-fabricated "Ready-Cut-Home" from a J.L. Northey, a friend in the lumber business, and joined forces with Mr. Redpath, another summer resident, to have the materials towed from Vancouver to the Point, where they had purchased two acres of property. With the help of some other friends they built two identical homes in the early months of 1919. Our house was painted white with red doors and windows and green trim. It looked like a Christmas tree compared to the other drab houses built along the beach.

Local materials—peeled cedar poles—were used only in the fencing around the entire two acres and for a flagpole. The pole sported a Union Jack that was religiously raised every morning before breakfast and lowered right after sunset. The flag had to be bent on the halyards every day, and my brother Bradley and I were taught to do this and assigned flag duties every week. Having served with the Territorials in Britain before emigrating to Canada in 1905, Father was intensely loyal to the British Crown.

The amenities at the cottage were few indeed. Kerosene lamps and candles supplied light. The kitchen stove supplied heat but most of it stayed in the kitchen, which was a very small separate room. Drinking water was carried in buckets from a near-by creek that tumbled down the hill just beyond the

property to the west. Washing water was usually available from two barrels filled by drainage from the roof. The nice soft rain water was great until it was decided to coat the asphalt roll roofing with coal tar. This was the wrong material to use because it is not compatible with asphalt roofing, and it polluted the water with a horrible taste and smell. Brad and a friend elected to do the roof-coating work, probably to earn a few extra pennies, but in their enthusiasm they unwisely painted moustaches on themselves with the black coal tar. Not only is this material smelly and toxic, it also burns skin badly. There was nothing in the camp to remove the tar until it had done its work—removing the skin. How those boys suffered.

Eventually Mr. Redpath decided we would dig a well and install a shallow well wing pump. A four-foot square hole was dug between the houses and cribbed with planks, many of them retrieved from the beach. The well, which was about fifteen feet deep, yielded water just as good as the stream and it never went dry.

At Gower our plumbing system consisted of an outhouse and a pit of sorts for the wash water. With no electric power there was no refrigeration and no electric motors of any kind. Actually there were no wheels in the area except the ones on the baby carriages and Harry Winn's Ford. The fastest things that went round and round were likely the egg beaters. The kitchen range for heating and cooking was fed with wood cleared off the property and driftwood from the beach. Dad did the heavy sawing with an old-fashioned Swede saw and the chopping with an axe that flew like lightning. Brad and I were responsible for splitting, piling and carrying the wood to feed the monster stove, the mighty Majestic. An empty wood box was a disaster of the first magnitude, with suitable punishment for the responsible or irresponsible urchin.

One of the problems with the stove was that the oven had a hole in the liner next to the firebox, so wood ash would often be sprinkled over the goodies that came out of it. But apart from its appetite for wood and the leaky oven the stove was a wonderful friend to sidle up to on a rainy day and dry your wet running shoes.

It may surprise people today that there was very little paper around in the twenties. The great paper mill complex at Powell River was not started until 1912. Fathers brought newspapers from the city once a week and these were used to bribe tugboat captains for apple pie. It was therefore necessary to have red cedar split very small or curled into shavings with which to start a fire. Since the stove often went dead more than once during the warm summer days a considerable quantity of kindling was needed. It is strange to remember that there were no coal-oil stoves or heaters in the house. They may have been available, but aside from the lamp oil no dangerous fuel or equipment was allowed in the house. Even the matches were carefully stowed away in tin boxes—the mice again.

Along the Gower Point waterfront around 1921.

Gower Point was actually not a point of land clearly defined by a coastal promontory, but a series of shallow curved beaches with only slight changes in rock formation and tree growth. Two large rocks seemed to mark the easterly and westerly boundaries of the settlement. They were located at approximately mid-tide mark and so were wholly or partially visible at all times. They were about a mile apart and it was within this distance that the summer colony spent July and August. To a small boy the rocks seemed ten or twelve feet high and twenty-five or thirty feet around.

In addition to being natural markers these rocks were, at low tide, a constant source of big, juicy green sea worms that could be gently pulled from their hiding places among the barnacles, mussels and seaweed. The three- to six-inch thorny- looking

worms were used for baiting hooks to catch perch, cod, bream and flounder off the float. Nobody had fishing rods with reels, and there were few gaffs or nets to help bring in the fish. We just tied the line to a short piece of green sapling pushed through a gap in the gunwale or onto a rowlock hole. When the sapling bent or wiggled we knew we had a bite. When the fish was finally in the boat it was also in the middle of a tangled line, which got even more tangled as the fish thrashed around looking for a way out. By the time the fish was subdued it took half an hour to get the line straightened out so you could resume fishing. This was not an expert fishing procedure but we did catch some fish.

A three-foot dogfish presented a problem one day when it was hooked and landed on the float. No one could summon enough courage to grab the hook out of its mouth and slit the monster's belly open, the common method of making sure it would never eat another meal. It was still thrashing around when two bold kids picked up a heavy iron cleat and dropped it on the fish's head. The two small eyes popped out and hit an empty wood box a few feet away with a sound like two marbles hitting a barn door. This seemed to discourage the dogfish and he gave up the struggle. Dogfish were the enemy of all fishermen and probably still are, because they would take a bite out of a nice salmon's middle and then slowly swim away.

Besides the two big rocks that served as punctuation marks, there was a big fir tree at the west end of the beach in what was called Amen Corner. This tree served as a guide or landfall for any boat returning home from the open gulf. It was easily the largest tree left from the logging operations. The bush and second growth trees that had sprouted some years before grew right down to the beach. Except for a grassy strip which pretended to be a road there was practically no flat land.

At the east end of the beach lived the Chasters in their honeysuckle-covered house. They were the year-round residents who took a kindly interest in the summer visitors. It is possible that at one time they had owned all of the Point and had sold it off in small parcels like the one Father bought. Harry Chaster was considered by everyone to be just below God. Without Harry the Point and its people would have been somewhat helpless. He kept them coming back year after year with his quiet smile and helping hand.

Some of the things the Chasters possessed were envied by small boys. One was a flat-bottomed skiff named *Sparrow*, a somewhat inappropriate handle because of its dead weight and lack of seaworthiness. But at high tide in the long warm summer evenings it was pleasant to row and scull the *Sparrow* in and around the creek estuary and then far up into the creek where the tide had made the water deep enough for quiet exploration. It was like having your own dream while being fully awake. These little voyages, made in complete silence with only the small fish for company, were treasured by anyone with an imagination, usually a generous commodity in the young.

Another Chaster treasure was a huge circular grindstone operated by a foot pedal or treadle. This relic was probably left behind by the loggers. They would use such a tool to sharpen their double-bitted axes razor sharp, then use the axes along with their six foot crosscut saws in the destruction of the forest. We used the grindstone regularly to sharpen our pen knives, which we used to cut and carve all manner of things, including ourselves. A knife rarely lasted more than one summer, so this item was always at the top of any Christmas asking list. In order to use the stone, one first had to ask permission and then outwit the white geese that guarded it.

The Chaster house around 1914.

The so-called domesticated white geese were nasty creatures that stuck out their long necks, hissed through their yellow beaks, and tried to nip off your toes. It was either a case of asking that they be locked up or working in pairs, so while one boy was sharpening his knife the other could be drawing them off by running fast around the yard. We could never understand why this marvellous machine was not tucked away safely in a workshop or a barn instead of being left out in the open. I hope someone rescued it and put it in a museum before it was destroyed.

Next to the Chasters' was a colony of school-teachers, many of them of Scottish descent, whom Brad and I often faced in games of golf. We would play with proper steel or iron clubs with wood shafts and a dime store solid rubber golf ball, while our opponents, steeped in the lore of golf as it was played on the Scottish links, played with wooden clubs fashioned out of tree roots and driftwood. They even made their golf balls out of wood. They were remarkably good with these crude tools, but not always good enough to defeat us with our dime store gear and youth on our side, though having spent no money on equipment they could afford to lose a little on the game. The so-called golf course was an arrangement of nine jam tins buried in the ground in a partially cleared area with pockets of sand, low bushes, small trees, and snakes as the hazards. The strokes you used to kill the snakes were not counted on your score but no one knew for sure when you were trying to hit the ball or trying to kill a snake. This worked for both sides. The idea of making money at a simple sport like golf and at the same time bringing down a boy's arch-enemy, a schoolteacher, was too good to be true.

The west end of the settlement was where the preachers lived, along with the Hamiltons, Bartons, Redpaths and ourselves, among others. Since Sunday morning services were held just outside the Reverend Wilson's house, this part of the Point was known as Amen Corner. If it rained the services were scrubbed, because not only would the congregation get wet but so would the squeaky little harmonium that was dragged out of the minister's house and played by his wife. Because of the lack of flat land the congregation of twenty or thirty were scattered in and around clumps of Oregon grape, salal, bracken, rocks and other obstructions.

The harmonium and the hymn singing were blessings in disguise. They permitted quiet games of crokinole, discreetly hidden in the bushes on the perimeter of the group. Crokinole consists of an octagon-shaped board about three feet in diameter with a small indentation in the centre guarded by rubber-covered pegs. The idea is to flip checker discs into the depression or behind a peg where an opponent cannot knock it off the board. A keen eye and a strong finger is all you need. Normally the game is played with shouts and arguments, but

remembering you were in church brought a certain amount of decorum, and all fights were put on hold until after the closing hymn.

There was one doctor staying on the Point. There may have been one at Gibsons, but in an emergency anyone seriously injured or ill had two choices: to be carried four miles over the trail to Gibsons or send a messenger for Harry Winn and his Model T truck. The box on the truck was no more than four feet long so you could not be stretched out straight. And the road, such as it was, consisted of two narrow ruts through the bush. Harry Winn's Ford was the only vehicle known to make the trip between Gibsons and the Point during all the years of our stay. In the summer he did it once a week to deliver groceries and other necessaries to the campers on a cash-and-carry basis. He brought only what had been ordered the previous week. Making up those orders by assembling requests from all family members was quite a problem for the mothers who, generally speaking, had little to spend.

Along with passing tugboats and visits by the steamships from the city, Harry's Model T, a veritable nervous Nelly on wheels, was guaranteed to cause much excitement among the kids. Harry might have been shaken up but he was always cheerful. Why not? He had a captive market and no competition, except reports by fathers of prices in the city. Little boys didn't think about commercial problems so didn't worry about how people like the Chasters and the Winns made out during the other ten months of the year.

The beach was rough and rocky with a stretch of sand only at extreme low tide. The sand was elusive because it seemed to move back and forth each year while advancing toward the mid tide level and then receding again. With no shelter whatever from east or west, there was always the danger of a dust-up in the gulf. Father trained us to keep a weather eye on the barometer for changes in pressure and to read the sky for squalls. We had no radio for weather forecasts.

It was because of the storms in the gulf that the beach yielded such treasures to those who would look for them. After each storm a gaggle of boys could be seen advancing along the beach for two or three miles each way from the Point. From a distance we must have looked like a string of crickets or grasshoppers, as the business of beachcombing was combined with a competitive sport involving the use of long, stout poles with which we vaulted from one log to another without touching the sand or the rocks. You had to stick to the log you landed on because if you fell off you went to the end of the line. Jumping poles were jealously guarded.

The treasures on the beach included various bits of flotsam and jetsam like shingle bolts, cottonwood bark for carving small boats and other objects, fish net floats, planks, mysterious boxes, wreckage from boats that had broken up in storms and a special

The Freezin' Follies. Dress rehearsal on the sand bar about 1921.

porous branch of a tree, never identified, that could be lit and smoked like a real cigarette.

On one occasion a dead horse was discovered lying at the high tide level. It had fallen off a ship at Gibsons and had been carried by the tide back and forth for a few weeks before ending up on the beach some distance from the settlement at the Point. With the wind blowing away from the settlement, inhabitants were safe from the awful smell of rotting horse—about on par with a live skunk. A fire was carefully lit with driftwood and the carcass was completely encased in flame. There was plenty of wood available to keep the fire going all day. Fortunately the wind stayed steady in the east and a smelly weekend was averted. On another occasion, a large dead seal arrived at about the same spot. Similar tactics were used but this time the fire was not as large. The argument as to which animal, horse or seal, smelled worse was never settled.

The biggest prize to wash up on the beach was found one Sunday morning with a heavy sea running and the breakers crashing in on the beach. It was probably the noise of the surf that woke us early before the rest of the residents were stirring. With the tide ebbing and already low it was possible we might find the elusive sand bar, so Father and I headed to the beach and to the west away from the cottages.

We didn't find the sand but saw something bright red bobbing up and down in the surf a few yards out.

On closer inspection it looked like a swamped red canoe but then we could see behind the red blob a long, bright metal cylinder. It was an unusual object, perhaps the most unusual that had ever been spotted. As it came in closer we could see a ring or loop in the nose cone, so I was sent home to find a length of rope so we could pull it free of the pounding surf to the safety of the beach. With the aid of small logs used as skids, we eased it onto dry land. Father and I became tremendously excited when we found double propellers and rudders at the tail end. The object, about two feet in diameter and twenty feet long, was clearly a torpedo.

Was it full of explosives, and was it British or German? The year was 1925, only seven years after the end of World War I. If the torpedo suddenly exploded, our house would be the first to go because it was closest.

While we were examining the deadly missile for clues, the community woke up to the danger and a small and curious crowd quickly gathered. Suddenly there was a puff of smoke from the front end that surely indicated something dreadful was about to happen. Nobody stayed to find out what that might be. Everyone vanished into the bush, behind logs and roots, or up the beach. One pair of boys went all the way to the next settlement before deciding it was safe to return home late that afternoon. The Reverend Wilson, barefoot, had his trousers rolled up on his white chalky legs, which moved up and down like tugboat pistons as he made great speed in an easterly direction. The speed was partly due to the fact that he was running over sharp barnacle-covered rocks that were exposed at low tide.

After a reasonable interval, maybe an hour, the residents decided it was safe to return to the torpedo and decide what should be done with it. Since Father and I had discovered it, it was considered our prize, although a dubious one. After much discussion and some sniffing, it was discovered the smoke had been generated by a little water coming in contact with carbide, similar to that used in our first bicycle lamps. This would signal the position of the torpedo at night on practice shots from a British cruiser, the HMS *Capetown*, which unknown to anybody had been cruising about in the gulf a short time before.

Father elected to go to Gibsons with Brad, leaving me to guard the prize. I was so dumb I didn't realize I might not be there when they got back. They sent a message to the naval authorities reporting finding one of His Majesty's torpedoes, twenty feet, steel, with a red nose to match the face of the torpedo man who lost it. There were visions of a big reward because it was obviously a lot more valuable than Harry Winn's Model T. The war was over but who knew when another one might start? They were still practising, weren't they? And torpedoes don't grow on trees.

The next day a motor launch moved quietly onto the beach at the Point, and spirited the tin fish away without saying anything to anybody. Later we found out from Mr. Craig, a friend of Father's who was in charge of the dockyard in Esquimalt, that credit had been given to the man who owned the launch. We were miffed about this because we thought we had rescued the missile from certain destruction on the rocks, received no compensation for running to Gibsons and back, and were not paid for the telegram. After that Father kept his Union Jack in the locker for a week. Eventually, though, we did get some acknowledgement. The Department of National Defence sent Father a cheque for five dollars.

Harry Chaster's choice of clinker-built Turner boats, and the admirable way he rowed them out to the steamers standing and facing forward in heavy seas, made it absolutely essential for anyone's father, if he had any sense, to buy a Turner boat too. Eventually, when he felt we kids could be trusted, Father did the right thing and surprised us with a brand new ten-foot Turner boat. He immediately set to work to paint it white with green and red trim to match the house. He also bought two pairs of oars and four oarlocks to develop young muscles. No newfangled outboard motors for him.

After a few years we became one with the boat and could row for hours, smoothly and easily, but not without a blister here and there. Our greatest expeditions involved rowing with the tide and, with luck, the wind toward any large or small tug pulling a boom of logs to the city. Two pairs of oars, a lookout bow man, and a stern man was a good group because one pie is easily divided into four. The *Sea Lion* was our favourite because of its huge size, its crew, and the delicious apple pie that awaited us in the galley. Since tugs were often many days at sea

The Sea Lion, *from which many apple pies flowed.*

with no radio communication we traded the latest newspaper we could get for pie. The deal was always made with the captain, who decided whether we could come aboard. We would tie up to the ship and climb aboard with the paper. First we would make our delivery and check to see the captain was on course, then we would slither down the hot steel ladder to the engine room. The big steam engines with pistons flying up and down were a little scary to us and the fireman who had to shovel coal into the boiler and rake the ashes out looked at us through two red eyes in a face of black. He always had a rag around his neck like Bogart in *The African Queen*, to remove the sweat and move the dirt around.

Some of us might have aspired to be tugboat captains or engineers on steam trains, but nobody wanted to work below deck on a tug slogging along at a snail's pace with hardly any fresh air moving through the ventilators. The job of cook had its attractions, but here again he was cooped up in a small galley with lots of big black pots and an even bigger coal-burning stove. If we were lucky, and we usually were, we each devoured a quarter of a pie before scuttling back to the boat for the long row home. Occasionally the cook might not benefit from or agree with the pie deal made by the captain, and he would object to our collecting for the paper and chase us off the boat, screaming and waving a large knife or meat cleaver. If he was Chinese he would not be able to read the paper, so you could not blame him.

One important rule we learned very early was never to attempt crossing behind a tug between the boat and its tow. A barge tow was be the worst because of the height of the towline above the water at each end. The towline drops very quickly into the water and if you are not careful it will cut you in half. At the other end where the cable comes up out of the water it will lift you and dump you right in front of the tow. On all of these tugboat visits there were undoubtedly a host of guardian angels flying about in case of misadventure. They were especially needed when we pulled in behind a log boom for a swim, and let the suction pull us along. If the boat or a boy fell behind, it would be a long swim or row home.

On all expeditions, by land or by sea, all adventurers were equipped with the basic weapon—a slingshot. The Y-frame was available everywhere, on the beach or in the bush, and we were always seeking the Holy Grail of slings. The leather pouch for the projectiles was filched from the tongue of an old shoe, and tough beans to any stranger who left his city shoes unattended. The rubber connections from Y to pouch supplied the power and were hard to come by at the Point. The usual source was an inner tube from an automobile or bicycle tire and there were none of these around. The auto tube was best because of its thickness and durability, but in those days people patched punctures themselves at the side of the road and put patches on patches, so it was hard to find a discarded tube that was serviceable. A strip carefully cut from an old tube to a width suitable to the operator's pulling strength was useless if it contained a patch or a thin worn spot. One of the principal excuses for a hike to Gibsons was to search around Harry Winn's premises for discarded tires and tubes. Why we didn't take a supply with us at the start of the season I cannot remember, unless it was because Father was always in charge of packing and unpacking and he had his ideas about carrying junk.

Generally the slingshots were used on inanimate objects like cans on a log or the large end of a log showing the annular rings and the central pith. In those days, before the forests were woefully depleted, a six-foot diameter log was not uncommon. The five hundred to one thousand-year history in one piece of wood was lost to boys bent on finding drifting treasure of another sort. Crows were considered fair game because they were noisy and did not appear to contribute to the overall scheme of things. We soon learned that crows had either their own built-in radar or phenomenal eyesight. They could spot a rock fifty yards away and just hop up or down on to another branch. As a matter of fact, we came to believe they could dodge a .22 calibre bullet unless it was fired from a distance of less than ten feet.

Among the few disagreeable creatures in Paradise were the snakes. They were probably harmless, but to some, particularly me, they were a deadly enemy to be annihilated as quickly as possible. The slingshots were brought to bear on these slithery creatures, especially when they were encountered on the beach. There was one group that congregated in a small area where the sea had receded leaving a patch of dry scrub, old logs, sea grass and other debris. This was home for the only black snakes in the area, about three feet long and one inch in diameter. Whenever you approached they immediately raised their bodies like cobras and gave you the evil eye. This was the moment when they got a slingshot projectile right between one evil eye and the other, if you were lucky. We were never successful in eliminating this group and the memory of them still brings on the shivers. One day, during my first year at the Point, a four-year-old girl who was staying with friends from the city for the first time went running to her mother shouting wildly, "Mommy, Mommy, I just saw a tail going alone." She had just seen her first snake.

The only beverages we had were tea, cocoa and milk. Coffee was not a popular drink in those days and there were no soft drinks at the Point. Since tea was not for children, that left only cocoa or water. With chocolate flavouring I could get the milk down, but under no circumstances could I stomach the stuff without some flavouring or camouflage. This dislike of milk came about because I was forced to drink it at school to pad out my bony ribs and knees. The

The Winn store in Gibsons.

milk was delivered to the school early in the morning and left on the sunny side until recess at 10:30. By that time the sun had turned the milk into something smelly, yellow and unpalatable. The school had no cafeteria and no refrigeration. It is surprising that everyone on the Point survived the lack of refrigeration and pasteurization of milk. Not even the Chasters, who were year-round residents, attempted their own electric generation that would have made this possible. Oil-burning refrigerators had not been invented. The only forms of energy were muscle power for work and kerosene for light.

The milk at the Point came from the black and white Holsteins and the brown Jerseys, owned by the Chasters, that wandered around the settlement like the sacred cows of India. The cows must have known about my resentment of their product because whenever I tried to pass them on the grassy road they immediately changed from docile, plodding creatures to menacing Spanish bulls. Not only did the cows lower their curved horns in the general direction of my trousers but they tried to cut me off from my destination. There might be five cows in the group so I was always outnumbered. To add insult to injury they often left large cowpads just where I might step in a dry pair of shoes.

Because of the shortage of feed and maybe for other reasons, the Chaster milk supply occasionally dried up. By some system of communication an arrangement was made for us to pick up milk at the leaning tree on the trail to Gibsons. This meant a hike of about three miles there and back nearly every day. The milk was in pails with a family's name on each lid. We eventually found out the milk came from a farm farther up the hill which was owned by a man called Steinbrunner. During the First World War and shortly after, Germans were not popular in Canada. We suspected the milk might be poisoned because why did the farmer just leave the milk then disappear? The method of payment was obscure and we supposed that some older person, maybe a spy, kept track.

Eventually the day came when there was no milk waiting for us at the leaning tree, so we courageously crept up a different trail to the farm fence and wondered if it was safe to go farther. The instructions were to bring home milk so we haltingly approached the farm sheds and were met with a bloodcurdling scream. Everyone in the party turned white and froze in their tracks. We were finally spotted by Mr. Steinbrunner, who explained his milk delivery plans had changed because he had to slaughter some pigs. The scream was the last complaint of one of the pigs. We got our milk and hurried home as quickly as possible. It was plain Steinbrunner had some large sharp knives in his possession, and one day he might run out of pigs.

Groups of about six of us, ranging in age from eight to twelve, often hiked to Gibsons. The only refreshments along the way were huckleberries and salmonberries. The former were small pink berries without much taste. They grew on bushes that sprouted from tree stumps. When logging was done with axes and long crosscut saws, trees were cut farther up off the ground than they are now. The loggers first had to cut notches into the trunk for the springboards on which they worked. Because of this

trees and left fallen debris mixed with fireweed, bracken, small bushes and fast growing alder. In more than ten years no attempt had been made to plant new timber trees to replace the ones slashed down, and even then it looked like it was too late.

Gibsons had only a few more houses than the Point but had two important facilities: a wharf and a store. There were usually letters to post if we had not lost them on the trail, and we had the agonizing task of deciding how to spend a dime or, if we were lucky, a quarter, if they were not lost too. A five-cent ice cream cone usually came first, followed by a nickel chocolate bar. There were essential items like fish hooks and line and spinners or a piece of sandpaper. There might be an errand of some sort for a mother who had not been able to visit the store in

One of the Union Steamship fleet, the Lady Cynthia.

extra height some bushes were harder to reach. The centre was often rotted out and made a fine place for new vegetation to take hold. The salmonberries were second best, like a poor man's raspberry, but acceptable on a hot day.

At one spot on the trail an overhead trestle of timber had been built down the hillside carrying a flume of planks. The flume was four or five feet wide at the top with slanted sides about three feet high, and when in use had been used to float cedar shingle bolts to tidewater from logging operations higher up the hill. Perhaps someone had corralled a water supply and diverted it down the flume, which may be why I remember no creeks on the route.

The entire area between the Point and Gibsons was a dismal one because of the logging operations. They had stripped the hillsides of all the beautiful

two months. Unless a boat happened in during our visit we could usually use the wharf to fish or swim. After a search for inner tubes and old shoes, we slowly retraced our steps back to the Point.

There was a sense of excitement every Friday night because that is when the fathers arrived from the city for the weekend on what the Union Steamship Company dubbed the "Daddy Boats." The weather was terribly important because we never knew if a father would step lightly off the ship on to the float, or fall in the water in an attempt to leap into a plunging rowboat, or be carried off to Roberts Creek six miles away. We knew he would have a meat roast in his bag and maybe some other small surprises for us, plus a newspaper for a tugboat captain. Because of the promise of fresh meat we boys worked like mad on Friday to make sure there was plenty of wood to feed the mighty Majestic stove to cook the Saturday dinner. There was always plenty for everyone to do on weekends but we were not allowed to do as we pleased on Sunday morning. Church was important to parents in those days and even when my father and I would go to the golf course on Sunday and play eighteen holes, we would return in time for church.

Saturday nights were for huge fires on the beach, maybe with roasted potatoes, and a sing-song after. Wood had to be gathered and made into a pile like a wigwam ready for darkness to fall. It was more like a distress signal than a simple campfire, but there was so much wood on the beach it seemed the right thing to do. One of the best things about the beach at night when there were no lights were the millions of stars, shining much brighter than they ever did in the smoky city. The beach faced west and the sunsets were truly magnificent, even to a small child. But quick boy, run and lower the flag, it's past sunset!

The opposite to the Friday night arrivals were the Sunday evening departures when the breadwinners returned to the city for another week of toil. The mothers almost never returned to the city with their husbands because they couldn't leave their brood alone for five days. The guardian angels were busy enough without taking on the job full-time.

After two months of swimming, fishing, beachcombing, hiking, playing endless games of crokinole, carving boats, chasing tugs, and listening to the surf and the wind in the trees, it was hard to think about returning to the city. But it was inevitable because two months were about all Mother and Father could take. It wasn't exactly a bed of roses for them. Perhaps they didn't know it, but we children would turn out to be eternally grateful. They would be glad to see us back in school, wearing laced-up black boots instead of smelly running shoes. The one pair of runners had to last the full two months and by the end of summer they were almost as bad as the skunk family we once found residing under the house. The skunks moved out on their own accord but the shoes had to be buried.

A definite routine was followed by Father in closing up the cottage. Nothing edible was left except the mattresses, which were rolled up and hung from the ceiling away from any rats or mice that might find their way in. All clothing, blankets and sheets were folded up and stuffed into a huge dunnage bag about five feet long. A few small suitcases took the rest. The boat was locked away under the house and shutters were screwed on over the windows. I believe the doors were barred from the inside and the final exit was made by a window, but this might not be true.

We were not sure what would have happened if it had been too rough for the steamer to land at the float loaded with several families and all their baggage. There was no place a group of families could stay even overnight without reopening the cottages. Anyway, the big red brick schoolhouse was waiting with its freshly oiled floors and musty atmosphere, just the opposite of the tremendous freedom of Paradise Point. We attended two schools: reading, writing and arithmetic inside four walls in the city, and Mother Nature's wonders at the Point with the

From left, Jack, Les Pope, unknown, Brad, Margaret, unknown, behind the house. Flag pole on the left.

sky for a roof. The sight of a squirrel in a tree or a big salmon on a line stay with you much longer than an algebraic equation or a chunk of English grammar.

In 1950, twenty-five years after leaving Gower Point for the last time, I drove my wife and two of our children to a ferry landing and we crossed Howe Sound to a new wharf near the old landing. Our car was a shiny new Pontiac and I was thinking as we flashed by the old wharf and what looked like Harry Winn's old store, that I could hear the chug of his Model T. Very soon we turned off the highway at a sign that read "Gower Point." The rocky beach came up more quickly than I had expected and we passed a modern one-storey house with a truck parked in the driveway. It looked like it was situated about where the Chaster house should be, but the vine-covered house was gone and there were no geese or cows to be seen. The salmon creek and its estuary with the small wharf was nowhere to be seen. This was sad because the stream was the birthplace of thousands of salmon every year. The road, now paved, continued past nondescript houses, many with carports or garages. There were no flat grassy nooks where you could play golf or pump a harmonium. We eventually came to two identical houses, undoubtedly the ones built in 1917, but they seemed to have shrunk with time into small cabins. All vestiges of paint had disappeared, along with the pole fence and the proud flagpole. I was certain the house on the left was *the* one but thought I would not want to live in it now. The small freshwater creek where we had collected our drinking water had apparently dried up and been filled in. There were now many more houses strung along the beach into the distance.

Since there were no fire hydrants on the roadway and no plumbing vents in the roofs of the houses, I assumed they still used the little outhouse in back.

They must have had running water from some source, probably from wells just like in old times. The little one- or two-holers could not be seen because the bush seemed to be engulfing the houses. Mother Nature seemed to be objecting to their presence and trying to cover them up. This combination of an archaic style of plumbing at the back with an eight-cylinder gas-guzzling car at the front was most incongruous.

I got out of the car and worked my way down to the beach but there were no familiar logs or landmarks to be seen. There were no boats lying across the logs and there were no ragged urchins waiting to go to sea in search of a steam tug.

The road was punctuated with wood power poles loosely strung with electric and telephone wires that ran into the houses. They would have no need for oil lamps or four-gallon cans of kerosene, at least not until the local public utility made it impossible for them to buy the juice.

I looked out to sea searching for the *Chilco* or the *Chasina* or anything with a black and red funnel but saw only a plodding freighter far out on the horizon, as far from the rocky shore as possible.

I turned the car around and slowly drove back to the ferry, not wishing to talk because I was unable to find what I was looking for and unable to tell my family anything about the Point that wasn't there. As we passed the modern house with the truck parked out in front I could see a mailbox on a post. The faded letters on the box read "Chaster." Had I dreamed the whole nine years or had there really been a Paradise Point? The name on the mailbox seemed to say, "It was here once, my friend, but Paradise is lost."

My brother and sisters still talk about it but they have yet to discover for themselves the dream is gone forever. Perhaps the magic of youth is not a matter of place but of time, like Brigadoon or Shangrila.

KEEP ON FISHING

ALAN HAIG-BROWN

A visit to one of the many fishermen's wharves that dot the BC coast from Vancouver to Prince Rupert will reveal that a high percentage of the seine boats are still made of wood, though the number of fibreglass, steel, and aluminum boats grows annually as new boats are built and old ones lost. The *Invercan No. 2*, built in Prince Rupert in 1941, sank in a storm off the west coast of Vancouver Island in 1985. The beautiful old hull of the *San Jose*, built by Arimoto at San Mateo Bay in Barkley Sound in 1928, ended up as a fire-gutted hulk on the beach at Ladysmith at about the same time. Louie Percich's classic double decker, the *Nanceda*, sank off Carmanah Light in the 1987 herring season. Some old

press of seiners was the *Chief Y*. She had the length and narrow beam of a classic 1920s Japanese-Canadian-built seine boat, but she was showing her age. Her many coats of black hull paint were chipped and blistered, her gunwales and dodger showed signs of rot, and she was streaked with rust from bleeding nail heads. The BC salmon fishery has a limited entry policy that requires an existing boat to be retired for every new boat built. The *Chief Y* looked like a candidate for replacement.

A fisherman wanting a new vessel would buy her, then take the licence and build a new boat with the same length but a much larger beam and capacity. The boat would then be sold to a buyer who might

The Bones Bay salmon fleet heading to the grounds for a Sunday night opening in August of 1945.

boats are partially lost to the wooden boat aficionado's pleasure by the addition of utilitarian aluminum cabins or other such heretical alterations. Still other classic old wooden boats, many of them no longer bearing expensive salmon licences, continue to work for owners who limp from season to season and bank payment to bank payment, with never enough money or heart to treat their boats with the respect and care they need and deserve.

Happily, a good number of owners value and appreciate the fine lines and dollar-earning potential of a well-maintained wooden boat. Such boats are now a minority in the fleet, but they are always a treat when found amongst their peers at dockside, or seen with gear in the water on the fishing grounds. Well-maintained boats like the *Good Partner*, built by Fenner and Hood in 1936, the 1927 Nakade-built *Race Rock*, or the *Zeballos*, built at the Menchions yard in 1918, deny the stereotyped designation "dirty old fishboat."

In the winter of 1985 my son and I were prowling the floats at BC Packers' Celtic shipyard on the north arm of the Fraser River. The yard has since been destroyed and given over to condominiums, but then it was still the winter home of a good part of the 520-boat BC salmon-seine fleet. Tied in among the

put a licence of lower value on her and use her for prawn, cod, or some such fishery. Or she might be bought with plans to add accommodations on the after half of her hull that until then had been reserved for working. With the commitment of enough time and money she could be made into a good liveaboard, or perhaps even a charter boat. But this was not yet to be the fate of the fine-lined vessel.

In May of 1985, before it was demolished to put up a parking lot, I sat at the window of the Marine View Cafe on Vancouver's famous old Campbell Avenue fisherman's wharf. As I finished up the overflow from my shrimp sandwich, I tried to puzzle out the name of the seine boat receiving major surgery under the orange tarp down on the floats. When I finished eating I walked down past the plants of the Billingsgate, Lions Gate, and Van Shellfish Companies to the float for a closer look. There was the *Chief Y*, stripped of paint. Her bulwarks and cover board had been removed at deck level, while the dodger and roof had been taken from the wheel house.

Owner Peter Ilic stopped work to introduce Mario Ursich, the shipwright in charge of the dockside rebuild. Peter was pleased that someone would recognize the quality of his boat and the work that he

The Zeballos *(foreground) enters Namu harbour in August of 1945. She was built in 1918 at Menchions and is still working.*

was doing on her. Peter had emigrated to Canada from Yugoslavia, the home of many of BC's Dalmatian fishermen, but he was from the interior of the country, and had only started his fishing career in Canada as a teenage crewman on the *Argent* in 1964. Six years later he became skipper of the *Oldfield* and a year later, in 1971, he bought the *Chief Y*. At that time the first licence limitations were being introduced in the fishery. He paid $40,000 for the boat, and within ten years the licence alone on this thirty-ton vessel would be selling for over $100,000. The *Chief Y* worked well for Peter, but she was too small for the lucrative roe herring fishery that developed in the 1970s and provided income for the larger seiners each spring.

In 1974 he bought his second boat. He kept the *Chief Y*, but sold thirty-one of the standard sixty-four shares to skipper Frank Perko in 1976. Peter's second boat is a classic seiner in her own right. She is the *White Swan*, originally the *Western Crusader* when built and launched for Captain Charlie Clarke by Menchions Shipyard in 1941. She was built with a two-cycle diesel engine that built up carbon when idling, then blew it out all over the net in flaming cinders when revved up. Charlie sold her within a year to the rapidly expanding Kyuquot Troller's Co-Operative Association for use as a fish packer. They renamed her the *Co-operator III* and kept her until 1956, when they sold her to the Bagonaviches in Prince Rupert. They in turn named her the *White*

Swan, repowered her with a Caterpillar diesel, and used her for dragging and seining.

Peter Ilic has maintained the *White Swan* well. Her wooden bulwarks were replaced with aluminum before he bought her. He has altered the cabin by raising the wheelhouse floor to give the skipper fore and aft visibility. This does away with the need for a flying bridge while at the same time providing a warm roomy wheelhouse with lots of space for the radars, sounders, sonar, loran, and radio telephones that have increasingly come to be the skipper's eyes and ears in modern fishing. But the hull and much of the cabin are unchanged on the *White Swan*, and she remains a credit to her designers and builders.

By age alone the *Chief Y* is a credit to her creators. In June of 1985, a month after he replaced her coverboard and cabin top, Peter had her hauled up on a marine railway. From her graceful timbered stern to her long, tapering bow—complete with a newly installed bow thruster—she was as pleasing to the eye as any yacht. Fresh white paint covered new wood and old wood. Out of the water her lines lent credence to Peter's claim, "She's built like a canoe, a hell of a sea boat. I remember going around Estevan Point in the fall of 1978. We were fishing dog salmon in Nootka. I had to turn back in the *White Swan* but my partner kept going in the *Chief Y*."

Peter remembers another time fishing in Tasu on the west coast of the Queen Charlotte Islands. A much larger boat had all her pilothouse windows

Salmon are brailed from James Wilson's Irene W *at Bear River in Johnstone Strait about 1948.*

The Western Mariner *brails herring into Fred Kohse's* Sleep Robber *from a 500-ton set made by the Menchions-built* Western Warrior *at Laredo Channel in February 1961. All three boats are still fishing. The* Western Warrior *was one of the few seine boats built with all sawn yellow cedar frames.*

In 1945 cotton seine nets with manila lines and Spanish corks were still pulled by hand.

By the mid-1950s the nets were being hauled aboard with hydraulic power blocks as on this American-built double decker, Pacific Raider. *The boat in the foreground is a power skiff used in the San Juan fishery to tow the net.*

By the mid-1960s all of the boats had been equipped with power drums to wind the net aboard. This group of boats had gathered for a special opening off the mouth of the Fraser River in 1988.

broken out as the mountainous seas crashed over the bow. The *Chief Y*, with her long bow and house set well back, kept going.

Close examination of the *Chief Y*'s planking shows a few nicks and scars but no sign of some of her more serious accidents. When she was owned by the Bell-Irving's old Anglo-British Columbia Fishing Company her skipper was Bill Logan. He tells of moving toward a rock bluff in the Portland Canal near the BC–Alaska border when the steering wheel came off in his hands. The *Chief* hit the bluff, bounced a couple of times, and had the forefoot knocked right out of her. They patched it up with canvas and went to Prince Rupert for repairs. Another time, when they were fishing halibut in Alaska, the boat spent two days on the beach before floating off on a big tide.

Some say that the *Chief Y* was the seine boat that travelled to Tahiti during the prohibition years to pick up a load of rum. But according to Willie Egland, this story did not involve the *Chief Y* but another seine boat, the *Haida Chief*.

The original owner of the *Chief Y* was Choichiro Yoshida. Choichiro was born about 1887 in a small town near Osaka on the Pacific coast of Japan. He was the oldest son of that village's leading landowning family – a family that traced their ancestors back thirteen generations and took pride in its ability to care for the village people in times of drought. It is this family history that is carried in the name of the

Chief Y. The name Choichiro can be translated as: Cho – leader or chief; ichi – first; and ro – boy. Hence the English name Chief Yoshida, or *Chief Y*.

After coming to Canada when he was about twenty years old, Choichiro went to work in the fishing industry. He worked for a time on the *Rose N* buying fish. By 1926 he was ready to have his own boat built with financing from Japan and a mortgage from the Canadian Fishing Company. The opportunities for Japanese in the BC fishing industry were extremely limited, particularly in seining. A few Japanese had herring salteries that they supplied with their own fleets. The large companies controlled licences that they would allow Japanese to use. It was such an arrangement that Choichiro had with Canfisco when he approached Tsunematsu Atagi to build the *Chief Y* in his boatyard at Scots Pond, near the Scottish-Canadian Cannery at the west end of Steveston on Lulu Island. Atagi had built some of the first seine boats in BC, starting with a numbered series of boats named *Quathiaski* for the Anderson cannery at Quathiaski Cove on Quadra Island. He would continue building at the yard until he and his sons were interned by the Canadian government in 1942 and their property was sold. The family cherry trees can still be seen along the dyke and several of the gillnetters built by the Atagi sons in the post-war years are still in the coastal fleet.

Choichiro's daughter, Tsuyako (Suzie) Nakagawa, was six years old when the *Chief Y* was being built.

57

Two classic and well-maintained seiners entering their fifth decade of fishing.

The latest in seine boat design and technology is represented by Bella Bella fisherman Bill Wilson's aluminum Shore-built Kynoc. She makes use of her hydraulic tilt stern to bring the fish aboard with minimal damage.

She has fond memories of going down to the ship-yard every day to watch the progress on the boat and drink Whistle pop. Hisao Atagi, who built some of the post-war gillnetters, remembers that his father, Tsunematsu, would rent a scow to buy fine edge-grain boat lumber from the mills in False Creek. The boats were launched bow-first because Scot's Pond was so shallow that even at high tide the boat's bow would have to be dragged through the delta mud before floating free.

After her launching, the *Chief Y* went north to the Canadian Fishing Company cannery at Tallheo near Bella Coola. There her job was to tow the long string of oar- and sail-powered gillnet boats out to the grounds, collect their fish every day, move the boats to new locations if required, and in any time left over, make sets for salmon with her seine net. The first year the *Chief Y* had a Norwegian skipper, but in the following years Mr. Yoshida ran her himself. His daughter, Tsuyako, remembers the trip north, with her mother cooking in the little galley located in the fo'c'sle between the bunks and the big three-cylinder Atlas diesel engine. Some years they went to Kimsquit and another year they went to Namu. But in the early 1930s, with all the anti-Japanese licence limitations, her father decided to sell the *Chief Y* and build a smaller boat. The seine boat had several owners, including Anton Stancic and Simun Cvitanovic, who later had the *Reel Fisher* built at Menchions and sold the *Chief Y* to H. Bell-Irving & Company.

Often boats that endure well owe this to the good care of a limited number of owners. The *Chief Y* has passed through many owners since Choichiro named her. After Peter Ilic and his partner upgraded her in 1985 she was sold again and then, through a trade, ended up in the possession of the J.S. McMillan Fisheries, who took her salmon licence for a new boat they were building. The *Chief Y* was then sold to James Chandler of Prince Rupert. She no longer has a salmon licence, but with care she will go on serving her owner well as her keel scribes another chapter in our coastal history.

The *Chief Y* is not unique as a survivor. In 1986 there were 36 boats still registered from the 153 that had been placed on the Vancouver vessel registry in 1927. Of the original 153 boats, 47 had been seine boats, and of the 36 survivors, 23 were seine boats. A number of factors contribute to this 50 percent survival rate. The wooden seine boats are strongly built, and most were built with diesel, or quickly converted to it, and thus avoided much of the fire danger that comes with gas. They have always re-quired a considerable capital investment, which has encouraged their owners to maintain and upgrade them. To build an aluminum boat in 1990 with the same earning potential as the *Chief Y* would cost about three quarters of a million dollars. But most important to the survival of the seiners have been the boatbuilders and fishermen of BC who designed, built, and fished these fine wooden boats that still make up the majority of the fleet.

My Experience with Greatness

HOWARD WHITE

WHEN I WAS A KID I wanted to be great. A great man. Didn't matter at what, my ideas changed daily on that score, but I just had this very sure feeling I'd be great at it, whatever it was.

As it turned out, I was right. I did get to be great at a number of things, or at least pretty great. But there are a lot of problems with greatness I never suspected as a kid, and the main one grew out of that fuzziness about the chosen field, or perhaps more accurately unchosen field, you get to play your greatness out in.

I guess the lesson greatness has taught me can be summed up in two simple points, two things they don't tell you about greatness in school that when you found out about them tend to turn the whole thing into a kind of hollow victory. Number one is that greatness is a lot more common than they would have you think. Number two is, the process of selecting outstanding people for public celebration is rigged against the vast majority of people who do truly brilliant, herculean, heroic things. There are all sorts of people locked in obscure struggle whose ultimate triumph we will never read about, who but for fate, might have demonstrated the same mettle on the world stage amid international acclaim.

Take me.

I'm a really unfortunate case, in that even my peers ignore my accomplishments because they're in fields where I'm the only guy there. For instance I am the undisputed world champion at catching the Langdale ferry from Pender Harbour in forty-seven minutes in a 1973 Volvo with no brakes and eight cases of books in the back. I proved this last Thursday.

The distance from Pender Harbour to Langdale is forty-eight miles so I must have averaged a touch under sixty, which isn't a qualifying speed at the Indy, but I'd give a lot to see A. J. Foyt try and duplicate my feat. For one thing, the stretch from Pender to Halfmoon Bay follows an old logging road. I know the guy who pushed it in, Art Shaw. He had one of these weird cats with the controls up ahead of the engine and a blade that lifted right up over the cab, and old Art was kind of a passive resister when it came to obstacles like rock knobs, skunk cabbage patches or big stumps — his strategy was to go around. A lot of the skunk cabbage patches have dried up and a lot of the stumps have since rotted down, but Art's loops are still there, immortalized in six inches of cracking asphalt. They have loops at Indy too, but I doubt they have reverse banks, changes of radius midway through and six-inch breaks in the pavement like the Sunshine Coast Highway does north of Halfmoon Bay. Most Pender Harbourites give themselves an hour and a quarter to an hour and a half for the Langdale run, and the all-time record, as far as I know, is forty-one minutes. But that was set in a new Porsche.

The thing about a 1973 Volvo is, this story takes place in 1984. Volvos are good cars. I've had two of them now. One '62 fastback that I bought off Walter Ibey for four hundred dollars in 1971, and this 1973 wagon I bought off Edith Daly two years ago. But there's one thing you have to keep in mind about a Volvo, and that is they're only built to last eleven years. The ads all say get a Volvo and it'll last eleven years, and that's true. But what the ads don't tell you is that immediately on its eleventh birthday a Volvo gives up like the one-hoss shay and becomes a deadly risk to anyone attempting to run a further mile.

I'd had a driveshaft out of this Volvo once and I'd replaced the clutch once and put a new set of used rotors and calipers on the front axle, but apart from some rattles and clatters and flaking-away fenders, it kept going pretty steady. But last January it had its eleventh birthday. The first clue was it abruptly started using a quart of oil a day. I noticed a black puddle underneath it the size of a medium pizza and traced the trouble to a loose tappet cover. I buttoned that up and it stopped using oil for about three days, when I found a puddle under it the size of an extra-large pizza. This time it was a front main bearing seal. Still not realizing what the car was trying to tell me, I spent a very unhappy day and a half installing a new seal. A few fill-ups went by without my needing to add oil, then I brought it home with the tappets clacking like the Four Horsemen of the Apocalypse and found the oil level right off the stick. I looked underneath, but there was no puddle.

Actually the first thing that should have tipped me off was the rear wiper conking out. The older Volvo wagons were famous for that deliciously luxurious rear window wiper — it had a lot to do with my buying one — and I had always been impressed at the way this frivolous extra kept stiffly wiping, long after other unessentials like the radio, heater, trunk latch and emergency brake had corroded into oblivion. Blind Bob Wolpert, who runs an illegal junk yard up by the Spinnaker Road subdivision and is something of a purveyor of the new urban mythology, told me a Volvo is no good once that wiper stops and should be immediately abandoned on the roadside, but I have never been able to admit the supernatural into my real life decision-making process.

Anyway, one day after the extra-large oil puddle I got tired of driving without rear vision and remembered to turn the hose on the now completely socked-in rear window. The water from the hose didn't have the slightest effect on it. I took a close look and discovered the entire back end of the car was coated with a tarry amalgam of black crankcase oil and dust about three-eighths of an inch thick. I had to use a paint scraper and gasoline to cut a peephole. The next time I took it out, with clear vision of the road behind me for the first time in a month, it all came home to me. The road behind me appeared clouded in a bluish mist, where the road ahead was bright and clear. It was hard on the twists and dips around Pender to see more than a car-length behind, but going up the mile-long straight stretch outside Halfmoon Bay, the bluish mist became an inky smog completely obscuring the Peninsula Transport semi I'd passed seconds earlier. Thwarted from leaking her vital fluids away onto the ground, the old girl was now spewing it out of the exhaust with the emphasis of a sick whale spouting blood. I knew it was over then.

Having realized this, I also realized it would be a waste of time to fix any of the innumerable things that started now going wrong at the rate of one or two a trip—a strange lumpiness in the rear brakes, a half-turn or so of slack somewhere in the drive chain so it jolted like a coal train every time you touched the gas, a buck in the motor that would express itself going up hills and act on the drive chain lurch in a most alarming way—I knew I was going to have to get it up to the car dump while it would still make the trip under its own power, but I kept waiting for something good in the eight-hundred-dollar range to show up in the *Coast News* want ads, and kept thinking I could get one more little trip out of the Volvo.

This was how matters stood at 9:30 the morning of March 11, 1984, when Jake Willett woke me up with a phone call wanting to know how come I wasn't in Horseshoe Bay to meet him for our work poetry reading tour of Vancouver Island pulp mills. I had been supposed to take the 8:30 ferry from Langdale, meet him in Horseshoe Bay at 9:15, then take the 11:30 ferry from Horseshoe Bay to Vancouver Island and drive up to start our tour in Gold River that evening.

"Jake, you wouldn't believe this, but I just slept through the alarm." This was a fair enough lie considering it was the first thing I said that day, but it wasn't so good considering we have kids who wake up at 7 and go to school at 8:30, which Jake knew. The truth was I'd forgotten about our rendezvous, and about the entire four-day reading tour, and had been sleeping in quite determinedly with a pillow over my head.

"There's another ferry at 10:30. Can you make that?"

Jake is perhaps the most organized and reliable person on the Pacific Slope of Western America, at least among the work poets. He would be constitutionally incapable of missing a ferry. My only hope was that, as a labour writer of middle-class origin, he would understand what a working-class thing this was I'd done.

"Sure Jake. No prob," I said. "See you at..." I made my voice sound convincingly alert, I thought, but it was still too early in the day to add 10:30 and 1.

"11:30," he said firmly. "Don't forget the books."

"Right."

In a way it was lucky I didn't have any time to think, or speak to my wife. It probably would have ended in bloodshed. This wasn't the first time I'd done something like this, just perhaps the worst time. I stuffed a spare shirt and toothbrush into my briefcase and bolted for the door patting down my hair. Mary stopped me with my wallet and watch, and a look made up of equal parts of pity and fury, not safe to kiss.

On the front porch I halted with a realization that this rather typical screwup had just taken on a truly horrifying dimension. There before me in the yard hunched my blighted Volvo. The sight chilled me. A poem I planned to read later that day, about the death of a logger, came into my mind:

events
in themselves ordinary,
in combination deadly...

Not only was I about to attempt the twisty morning run to Langdale in a completely unrealistic time, I was going to try it in a disintegrating eleven-year-old Volvo that was unsafe to sit in let alone drive, and not only was I going to ask God to forgive me this temptation to fate, I was going to load the car up with eight heavy cases of books. I couldn't take my wife's good little Toyota, because I would have to leave it parked four days at the Langdale terminal and her constitution couldn't support life for over thirty minutes without her Toyota.

The logical solution was to have her drive me and I could sense she was just waiting for me to fall to my knees and ask, but somehow the trial presented by the Volvo, with its risk of almost certain death, seemed easier to face.

Going over the first hill I discovered the lumpy rear wheel brakes had now totally given up, leaving me with brakes only on one front wheel, which not only failed to much alter the car's forward momentum, but almost ripped the steering wheel out of my hands and pitched me into a granite bluff. So now in addition to making the hour-long Langdale run in an unsafe wreck overloaded with books, I was going to do it with only one locking front wheel for brakes.

I recognized that this was going to be one of the greatest tests I'd ever faced, one that demanded every ounce of concentration, of heroic nerve, that a person could ever be expected to muster. I snuck up carefully on the big hills, coasting over their crests at a near stall, nursing my shred of braking capacity along as far as I dared test that shrieking, shuddering left front wheel, then letting the old beast fly sixty, seventy, eighty miles an hour, making up the time I lost bucking up the grades at the head of my ever-thickening black storm cloud of oil smoke.

I stopped religiously every ten miles to throw another quart or two of oil into the smoking hot motor, no doubt setting the world speed record for pouring two quarts of oil too, and kept my ear so attuned to every new rattle and throb I was able to just keep the motor on the edge where I was getting everything it had left without giving it the excuse it desperately wanted to pack up totally. Talk about living on the edge, no Edmund Hillary inching along a Himalayan ice shelf was ever so exposed and vulnerable as I was streaking through the intersection at the bottom of the Norwest Bay hill in that smoking pounding missile of rust, grease and steam. And yet I was on top of the problem. Nothing caught me by surprise. When an elderly woman in a fifteen-miles-an-hour Pinto pulled out in front of me on a corner with a car in the oncoming lane, I just cranked it for the shoulder and streaked past, skidding in the gravel. If I had given in to the instinct to even touch the brake, that left wheel would have jerked me into the oncoming car so fast no one would ever have

62

known what happened. There were a hundred factors, all matters of life and death, which I had to keep juggling in my mind, never missing a one. I even remembered to slow down at the speed trap outside Sechelt, letting the Pinto overtake me and get nailed. Does an astronaut at his bank of blinking controls have so much to keep track of? No, all his equipment is forgiving and reliable and all his decisions neat and simple. Gus Grissom would never have made it past the hairpin at Silver Sands. But I made it to the ferry with thirty seconds to spare.

As it happened, there was a two-sailing wait and cars were lined up for a mile, but after what I'd been through nothing the BC Ferry Corp could throw at me could give me even a moment's pause. I just pulled into the oncoming lane, leaned on the horn and streaked through the lineup, yelling at the fluorescent-gloved attendant, "Emergency work—poetry mercy run! Gangway!", drove up in front of the baggage van and had six boxes moved before the fat lady from the toll booth had time to come puffing down.

"What do you think you're doing! You get back to the end of the line!" she barked. I smiled sweetly.

"Just loading baggage, ma'am."

Her buggy eyes followed the boxes from the drooping, dripping, hissing Volvo to the otherwise completely empty baggage van.

"That's not baggage! That van is reserved for hand baggage!"

"Are you telling me there's no room, ma'am?" I was done anyway. Her bosom was heaving under the blue Ferry Corp blazer as she struggled to contain her outrage, and before she could think up another institutional imperative to fling at me, I was into the car and gone back up the road. I just ran the old heap into the brush outside the compound and left the keys in it. Then I made for the ferry at a dead run.

It wasn't until I was leaning over the rail as the boat pulled away, watching the toll booth lady still waving her arms and regaling the man with orange gloves, that I let go. Waves of relief washed over me. I beamed at the luminous prop wash, the pale blue terminal buildings, the left-behind lines of cars, the dark slopes of Mount Elphinstone behind. And I just felt—great.

they don't make 'em anymore

GORDON BALLENTINE WITH PAUL STODDART

I WAS BORN IN VANCOUVER in 1905. Around the time I was at UBC – it was over in the old shacks where the Vancouver General Hospital is now – I began to get interested in airplanes. What started it, I don't know. I had made models and done all the usual things, and I think the first airplane I saw was during the first World War when I was very young.

Somewhere around '23 or '24 I made social contact with the young pilot officers who used to come out here from Camp Borden, Ontario, to do three months of seaplane and flying boat training at Jericho Air Station. We played together, swam together, drank together, and went to parties together, and I had my first airplane ride with a couple of fellows in a flying forest called an HS-2L Flying Boat.

Then there came the problem of how the hell do I get into the business because, in those days, civil aviation out here was nearly nonexistent. I had no money, so even if there had been a school I couldn't afford to go to it. Somewhere around 1926 various aero clubs began to develop and somehow or other I got involved with one of them and met Don McLaren, who ran an outfit called Pacific Airways Limited. Major McLaren is what we called him. In December of '27 I persuaded him to hire me, which he did in January of '28, for ten dollars a week.

This was absolutely great as far as I was concerned; this was the end of the rainbow! I don't know

if you ever wanted something like young guys wanted airplanes in those days, or somebody like me anyway. Don McLaren knew I wanted to be a pilot but my job was what was called a crewman. We used to have to walk the wings to steer the plane into the dock by dipping one wingtip float or the other, because nobody had thought to invent the water rudder to attach to the floats. I guess I was worth ten dollars a week for that. I was also a grease monkey and everything else. We got quite a bit of flying with co-operative pilots, so we learned a lot.

That winter and spring were taken up with re-building a Pacific Airways H-boat, which is what we called the HS-2L. We took it down into small pieces, did everything necessary, and put it all back together again. That was where I met Harold Davenport, who was Don McLaren's air engineer. I was a very lowly critter but a few charter flights came along and I went as a crewman. Sometime that spring Pacific Airways, Don's outfit, was purchased by Western Canada Airways out of Winnipeg.

That injected some money into the operation for the first time and they bought a Boeing A1D which was built in Seattle. That one crashed that summer and killed the engineer. We got several B1Es which were slightly larger and much better planes all around. They were closed in, had windows that cranked up and down, upholstered seats and all sorts of fancy goods. We got a Vickers Vedette and still had the

Pacific Airways HS-2L after being re-built in March 1928, at the foot of Bute Street.

Vickers Vedette G-CASW at Western Canada Airways fisheries patrol base, Swanson Bay, August 1928. The plane crashed the next day.

HS-2L where you sat where God meant airplane drivers to sit—out in the noise, cold, wind and wet.

I was assigned to go on fisheries patrol in June or July of that year. We went up to Swanson Bay, which was the main base for the northern patrol. It was chosen because it was an abandoned mill which offered buildings and sheltered mooring for the aircraft. It was quite an operation that year. There were something like five aircraft at anchor there at one time. We lost two that summer: the B1-D that I mentioned, and the Vedette—with me in it.

Not being the pilot, I didn't know exactly how it happened, but having become a pilot since, I'm pretty damn sure how it happened. It comes from trying to fly in cloud with nothing better than a carpenter's level for an instrument.

I was assigned to go over to the Queen Charlottes with a pilot named Neville Cumming and an air engineer named Alf Walker in the Vedette. We went up to Prince Rupert, overnighted, and started off for Queen Charlotte City. It was a grey sort of day. When you could see beyond the islands across Hecate Strait the grey sky and the grey seas started to blend. We were flying between two islands and all of a sudden we were in clouds. I was in the front seat, which is a sort of round bathtub affair, and Alf, who was senior to me, chose the better seat next to the pilot.

We were between these two islands and I assumed we would simply break out over the ocean, which is probably what the pilot thought too. The first thing we saw—at least the first thing I saw—was the tops of trees that looked about three hundred feet high and ten feet below us.

I must say that's a shocking experience. Neville poured the coal to it and started to climb but what manoeuvres we went through it's impossible to say because we were staggering around the sky. Every few minutes—I didn't know if they were minutes or years—I'd see the trees again. Eventually we got above the trees and smacked into the top of the mountain. There must have been a very loud crunch, although the people who are in these things never hear them.

The first thing I did was get out and stumble about fifty feet, thinking about fire, and fall down on my knees. I turned around and saw the plane was a pile of junk. It was a pusher plane and the air-cooled engine, normally in a vertical position, was flat like a pancake and still running. The gravity tank with three or four gallons of gasoline had ruptured and the gas was coming off the engine in clouds of steam. Why the thing never blew, who can tell?

Finally I decided I had to do something about the situation. I had to go around to the rear of the thing and crawl through something like a barbed wire fence—a bunch of splintered wood and wire. I reached the cockpit and the pilot, Neville, was sitting with his head slumped down on his chest and blood all over his face. Alf, who was sitting on the right, looked as if his face were made of chopped liver. He was dead as far as I was concerned. I was just

Vancouver 1935, seaplane base. Eastman Flying Boat (Detroit Sea Rover E2) CF-ASW Curtis Challenger engine, four-place.

Swanson Bay, August 1928, fisheries patrol. Rear — Bill Faulkner, crewman, Neville Cumming, pilot, Alf Walker, air engineer. Front — Gordon Ballentine, crewman, Major Donald R. McLaren, Harold Davenport, air engineer. Cumming, Walker and Ballentine crashed on Porcher Island the next day.

reaching in to switch off the engine when Neville made a reflex action and knocked the switch with his hand. His head flopped down again. I decided he must be alive if he could do that, but Alf was definitely dead. You don't have any feelings about it at the time. You're alive, so what the hell. These other poor buggers? That's their affair.

In my bathtub front seat was the emergency gear, with axes and food and all that sort of stuff. I crawled out through all this junk again and went around to the front, but I couldn't get into my seat because it was such a tight fit. The top wing had come down and cut my seat in two but somehow it hadn't even touched me. I dragged the stuff out, got the axe, and started back on the same route to the pilot's seat. I got there and the dead man was gone! I thought, "Well, God, he's going to be stumbling around the mountain, out of his mind," and we were in thick cloud, which is why we'd hit the mountain in the first place. I went back outside again, around to the front, and met this apparition coming the other way with his face a mess of blood and his hands all bloody. We stood and looked at each other and both started to laugh. A hysterical reaction, I guess. I was relatively undamaged. I turned many colours of blue and green over the next week but apart from a lost tooth and a few abrasions, I was in pretty good shape.

Alf put his hand out, obviously wanting a cigarette, but not being able to get his hands into his pockets because of all the blood. I fished out a cigarette, poked it in his mouth, and the damn thing disappeared. That was another shock! I thought I'd poked it right through his palate. It turned out that he and Neville had both been hit on the back of the head by the struts from the engine when it came down. Their faces had been smashed into three quarters of an inch of mahogany plywood, the instrument panel. In the process Alf's false teeth had been knocked somewhere into the bilge.

Alf and I organized ourselves. We had to do something about the pilot who had put us into this horrible position, though quite frankly, we didn't much care. Later, after I became a pilot, I often wondered how close I came to making people feel the same way about me. We couldn't lift the engine so we chopped the hull out from underneath and got him out that way. We stretched him out a few feet from the plane, then dragged him farther away because it was still possible the plane might burn.

He was a mess. He had a split in his head about five inches long and a half an inch wide. Really gruesome. His nose was smashed in and we didn't know if he was going to last or not. Also, we didn't know where we were. We didn't know if we were on an island, or the mainland, or where. We took turns wandering around but being careful not to lose ourselves and keeping what was left of the plane as our focal point. We had crashed around noon; at around five o'clock we could finally look down

through a hole in the clouds and see water. We didn't know what it was, but it was better than where we were. We still had this guy who refused to die, and we had to look after him, so we built a stretcher. We cut down a couple of poles, which were hard to find because we were above the treeline. We were just about to put the stretcher together with Neville's hunting coat and my leather jacket, when Neville came to and wanted to know what the hell was going on. We said we were going to carry him down the mountain.

"You're not. Where am I?"

He said we weren't going to carry him, that he was going to walk. Walk he did. It was the most amazing display of sheer guts. I came to respect him very much because he must have been in agony. He had on a pair of plus-four golf pants and low shoes, and his shins had been cut right to the bone. The two of us supported Neville and we stumbled downhill, which was something like coming halfway down Grouse Mountain at midnight without a trail. One of us would go ahead to try and find a usable route, then he would come back and the three of us would go down, then the others would go first.

About two in the morning we got to the beach and laid Neville out on a bed of branches. We were pretty beat. We tried to light the usual tree fire signal for distress. We'd get one lit and then the tide would come in and put it out, so we'd light another and the tide would come in and put that out too. Great boy scout stuff! I was born and brought up on tidewater but I forgot it came in. We got the third one lit and Alf and I stayed up all night signalling offshore, not seeing a light, not seeing a damn thing, which wasn't surprising because when daylight came we found we were in a little bay with an island covering the entire mouth of it. We'd been signalling to a vacant island all night.

The next morning the weather was nicer but we still didn't know where we were. We didn't know whether to go left or right or what. We tossed a coin to see whether it was going to be left or right, tossed another to see if it was going to be Alf or me. It came out that Alf would go to the right. I started to get some material together to make a raft because you can't drag people around on those shores; you just can't walk on them. I was going to tie it together with strips off my leather jacket, which was my pride and joy, but I had not yet made the fatal cut when Alf came back, two hours later, with his eyes all bugged out. Here was another tough customer, I'll tell you. His nose was broken, his face was all chopped up, yet he hadn't whimpered all night coming down that mountain.

He said he had got down the beach half a mile or so and there was a launch at anchor in the bay. He yelled and shouted and whistled and threw rocks but couldn't raise anybody because there was nobody on it. He went a little farther and came to a trail up the hill, which he followed for a hundred yards, and there was a telephone on a tree! Oh God! So he cranked this thing and you can imagine Alf's feeling and the feeling of the people on the other end.

"Where am I?"

"Where are you? Who are you?"

It turned out it was the beach site for a mining company and we were on Porcher Island. They came down the hill and said they'd get a boat and come around and pick us up. Lo and behold, this big rowboat comes around the point an hour or so later and out of it get three guys I'd gone to university with the year before: Ross Tolmie, Hugh Woodworth, and Doug Telford. They took us into Prince Rupert on this launch. Alf and Neville went to hospital and I took the glad news back to Don McLaren at Swanson Bay that he was short an airplane.

He flew me up over the crash site the next day and we organized a salvage party to go get the bits and pieces. After this crash, I remember McLaren asking me for my opinions on the emergency rations, and would it have been better to have a bottle of brandy with the rations? My answer was that brandy only would have made us thirsty. One of the odd things about the rainy north coast is that it's sometimes very difficult to find a drink of water, and after climbing down that mountain we were thirsty. All I could think of that night was thirst.

After spending a week on the salvage party I went back to Swanson Bay and was assigned to another

pilot and plane. Alf and I went over to the Queen Charlottes and spent a month over there on fisheries patrol. While we were there the HS-2L blew its engine. Davenport had been up on the lower wing feeling the engine for hot spots, hot cylinders and so on. He had just got back to the cockpit when the thing blew and sent shrapnel right to the end of one wing, cutting it up so badly it wasn't worth anything. Besides, with more money available, who the hell wants an HS-2L? They had become obsolete ten years earlier.

In 1929, Davenport, McCurdy, and I lost our jobs. I lost mine because I wasn't getting to be a pilot fast enough, but I don't know why they lost theirs. Art McCurdy—who'd been an air engineer with Western Canada Airways—and Harold Davenport started a ground school in Vancouver on 4th Avenue, and after a couple of months I joined them. Harold taught engineering, Art taught rigging and woodworking, and I taught theory of flight. We would get the students to build a glider, then we'd sell it to get the money for more materials and more students. We made one to sell but the deal fell through and there we were, stuck with this glider. There was a glider club around and we had a deal with them to use our glider under our supervision. Eventually we took over the operation and it became our school. We taught people to fly primary gliders,

August 1928. Gordon Ballentine on a salvage trip to the Vedette crash site on Porcher Island.

first at Lulu Island, then over at Sea Island back before the airport opened. We were the second or third tenants at the airport.

Our goal was to get into something bigger and better and we eventually ended up with powered aircraft and a proper flying school. Because we had our own school we both got our pilot's licences.

By the time we got the school together I think I'd only had about three or four hours of formal dual flying before I went solo. I'd learned a great deal about piloting while I was still a crewman. Most of the boats had dual controls; I'd watch the pilot and sometimes he'd let me fly it. You gain knowledge by osmosis, so instead of ten or twelve hours of dual I had three or four. For a commercial licence you have to have fifty hours solo. I think I was teaching flying at fifty hours and ten minutes.

Because people allowed me to fly their planes, I got onto bigger and better ones, so I got better and better jobs and went to straight charter flying. We had a co-operative thing called Aircraft Charter Services, which was mostly a booking service with a bit of charter work. I had some control over an Eastman Flying Boat because I'd taught the owner to fly. Hal Wilson had a Fleet Sea plane and Adam Richardson had a Boeing B1E. Each was a different size: I carried three, Hal one, and the Boeing four or five.

Back then the only outfit that insured planes was Lloyd's, and it was my impression that to a great degree they controlled who flew what. A pilot who had a bad record with Lloyd's couldn't get a job, and I can still remember the thrill I got when a guy offered me a job at ten bucks an hour, as pilot of a brand new Stinson. No salary, just ten bucks a flying hour. It was great to get the job, and have it on record that I was capable of that sort of thing.

You would look at a lake or a field, and only your own background and experience told you whether you could get on the lake and get off again, or on to the field and off again. This meant that there was a good deal of trial and error, because how do you know what's the shortest lake you can get out of until you've tried it? How do you know what the biggest wave is until you've tried it? You get pretty close to the edge, but you never become 100 percent efficient, because that means at some point you would have to bust something in learning what the maximum is.

In 1937, in the fall, the Zeballos gold rush got heated up and Canadian Airways started to get busy. Zeballos had been a prospecting area for a long time before that, but in '37 they struck enough gold to make a town out of it, a real gold rush town. At that time Canadian Airways had one pilot in Vancouver and one airplane: Molly Small and a Balanka Pacemaker. I pestered Punch Dickens, who was the General Manager in Winnipeg, for a job. Employment with Canadian Airways was the goal for all the pilots because it was the biggest bush company in Canada, therefore the most stable. I got the job and we ran a regular schedule back and forth, Vancouver to Zeballos.

When we first started going in there was no dock, no floats to the shore, no nothing. You anchored off a long, shallow, sloping beach and you learned to wear hip-waders. A fellow by the name of Major Nicholson, the postmaster, and his son used to come out and piggyback everyone ashore. It was a very busy period and there was a lot of competition and a lot of bad weather. It rained like hell over there, and there was mud up to our knees, which meant that everything in town was muddy and gritty.

The first hotel in Zeballos was the Pioneer, whose proprietor was Les Browne. It had some rooms, but if I had to overnight it was usually in the ram pasture, just rows of iron beds with grey blankets on the wide open second floor. Then a new hotel, the Golden Gate, was built right on the waterfront. It offered real luxury. Toilets in the rooms, even. But the Zeballos mud soon had the floors all gritty.

I saw the first gold brick shortly after it was poured on New Year's Eve. It had been brought down by the BC Provincial Police, who were guarding this thing before it was put on the plane. We'd get the bricks to Vancouver and one of the express companies, bonded and armed, would come and meet us to relieve us of this tremendous responsibility. Of course it was fairly common to get weather-bound at Tofino or Ucluelet, or any place in between, and the brick would sit on the float or in the plane unguarded. They finally woke up to the fact that the Royal Mail was sacred, at least in those days, and all they had to do was buy enough air mail stamps, put the gold in a blue air mail bag and quit worrying about it. These things would show up at the dock at Zeballos and be dumped there ready to be loaded on the plane. When we got down to Vancouver we'd throw out the mail bags and we'd know that the one that went "thump" was the gold. That was my first and only experience with a gold rush. We had prospectors all over the place and we used to take them in and drop them off with all their supplies and pick them up later. For a lot of them it was a holiday.

I might say that the period around 1938 was the turning point for aviation out here. It might even have been Zeballos that triggered it. Before that, there had been a number of efforts to get a permanent flying business going, but they'd just run for a little while and fold. Attempts had been made at a Vancouver–Victoria run but that was unsuccessful too. Finally Zeballos gave an impetus which was very much needed. It justified putting in equipment out here, and in serving Vancouver–Zeballos we also served Ucluelet, Tofino, Nootka, Friendly Cove, Port Alice, and others. This was just the trigger that was needed and I think that was the start of several flying services that ran on a continuing basis, including the Vancouver–Victoria run.

I was on fisheries patrol as a pilot during the summers of '38 and '39. By this time, instead of the five flying boats we had in 1928, we had one plane to do the Northern District from Cape Caution

Pilot Ballentine with Air Travel and Transport Ltd.'s new Stinson at Vancouver seaplane base in August 1937. AT & T had two planes—the other a Waco "C" with Ted Dobbin as pilot.

to Prince Rupert and another for the Southern District of Cape Caution to Nanaimo. I had the north route.

There are your trollers who can't poach at all—the fish have to go and bite their hooks to get caught. There's the gillnetter who just sets his net in the water, hoping the fish will run into it. He could poach by fishing during a closed period or in a closed area, and he had one trick we had to watch for: if he tied one end of his net ashore he could partly block a channel and get more fish. But it is the purse seiner that can circle a school of fish, pick up the entire school, and wipe out the salmon run in that creek for years. So the poachers using purse seiners were our prime target.

We learned all sorts of tricks. That was the fun of the thing, you were left to be as smart as you liked. Walter Gilbert, my boss at the time, used to send us young guys up there because it was an absolutely marvellous way to learn the coast and coastal flying. When first assigned to the job, you might be a little apprehensive because the fellows who'd preceded you weren't above telling tall tales of bullying inspectors, 3,000 foot downdrafts, and the like. But it didn't take long to learn that one inspector wouldn't fly in fog but hated rough air, another the reverse, and none of them were in any more hurry to get hurt than I was. Good fellows, all of them.

That was the most delightful flying job I ever had. Probably the poorest paid, but the most fun. We'd start late June and go until November. I served under one inspector whose job it was to assign me to five others on the coast, each of whom were entitled to a share of my contract flying time. I was deputized as a fisheries inspector so I could arrest people. About two-thirds of the time an inspector would come along with me and my mechanic, but the rest of the time he would simply assign me to patrol areas on my own. Actually, arrests were few and far between and it was a preventive service more than anything else.

There were no passengers, which can be the biggest worry for a professional pilot because he's responsible for getting them safely to where they want to go, or at least to food and shelter. Our only passengers were the Fisheries people, who were really part of the crew. We carried everything in the aircraft for our needs and comfort, including my office typewriter and files. We had guns, fishing tackle, food, sleeping bags, everything we needed to be at home wherever we landed. You can't imagine the feeling of freedom this gives you when you're flying for a living. I had a pad on my knee the whole time, writing down all the places we patrolled, and if I was out overnight I would type up the reports in quintuplicate. One of our inspectors, Gordon Reade, who would be called an environmen-

The hardships of Fisheries Patrol, 1938. The plane is a Bellanca Pacemaker.

talist today, insisted I use all the old Indian names, so every time I got a new map I had to ink in all the Indian names.

In a way we were just playing cops and robbers with airplanes. I guess 99 per cent of the fishermen saw poaching as a simple business risk. If they were caught, tough luck, but no bad feelings, no rough stuff. Good people. Our worst case was a white man from Europe who created a lot of trouble one summer and even took a shot at a couple of Fisheries people. I was out looking for him for quite a while but he was an elusive character. There was some violence before they nailed him.

One of the tricks we learned was that if we flew close enough to the thickly timbered hillside, the noise from our engine would be absorbed by the forest, and we could sneak along and drop down on some poor poacher. One time I had an inspector on board and we were sneaking along the ridge of a mountain, right close, and I could see this guy with his net set in the mouth of a creek. We landed, taxied up slowly to him, and the inspector said, "You haven't made an arrest this year. You'd better make this one." I didn't want to make an arrest. I was there to fly airplanes! I tied the plane up to the seiner while the fisherman pulled in his net. He was standing with his back to me, near the very noisy winch and he was seven feet tall if he was an inch. I finally had to tap him on the shoulder and say, "You're under

arrest." He turned around and was as shocked and scared as I was. He was a nice guy. A couple of years later, while I was sitting on a dock waiting for my charter passengers, he came up to me. We started talking and had a cigarette together. He kept looking at me in a funny way and finally said, "You don't remember me, do you?" I didn't. "You arrested me up at so and so."

Generally speaking there were no hard feelings. We did our job and they did theirs. If we were in a cove we'd often tie up to a seiner and perhaps even stay aboard for a meal or a smoke to wait out the weather.

We were all coastal people, and for anybody born and brought up out here, coastal flying was the only kind of flying you knew anything about or were interested in. We were trying to serve the coastal community and we had no weather systems at all, no reporting, no radio, no nothing.

One of the things that used to amuse us was when guys would come out here from the prairies to fly. They'd look around here on a fine day, see all these mountains, and say, "How the hell do you find your way around with all these mountains?" And we'd say "How do you find your way around without them?" They were landmarks to us. Prairie pilots' landmarks were railway lines and section lines which were just as foreign to us as the mountains were to them. The first time I flew east of the Rockies to

Fort St. James, January 1939. Gordon Ballentine's Bellanca Pacemaker and Russ Baker's Junkers.

Fort St. James, March 1939. Pilot Gordon Ballentine and a Pacemaker CF-BFB.

Edmonton, if it hadn't been for the railway line, I never would have found Edmonton.

There was very little formality about flying in those days. You started out to do a job and nobody worried you if you didn't have a radio. You came home, hopefully with your pockets full of money, as Gilbert used to say. Flying in those days was very much a one-man affair and just a great way to live. Walter Gilbert was a particularly fine man to work for. He used to pretend to be quite tough but he had a very soft heart.

In 1939 I had a mechanic by the name of Roy MacDougal on Fisheries patrol. One beautiful sunny day when we were headed for Prince Rupert, I said, "How'd you like to see where I left a plane here ten or twelve years ago?"

We altered course and flew over the site, then down into Rupert. We landed at one of the long docks and were tying up when someone came down and told me I had a phone call. It was a call from one of the newspapers saying a CPR steamer captain had just reported an airplane going down in flames over such and such an island. I thought for a moment and said "I think that was me and I think he saw the sun flashing off my prop. I certainly didn't see any other planes around." I went back to the plane and no sooner got there than I got a call from the other newspaper. Same story. Same answer. Got back to the plane, another call. This time it was the Lloyd's Insurance agent. So I said, "If you'll clear it with Gilbert, I'll go out and spend a half-hour of his money and see if I can find anything."

Roy and I took off and flew around. Sure enough, there wasn't a sign of anything, so I went back and phoned the newspapers and Lloyd's and forgot about it. However, word had spread up and down the coast about this airplane going down in flames, and since we were the only ones up there it had to be us. My wife was at Bella Bella, our base that summer, and we'd only been married a year. There was a little Air Force station there and they had got the word but didn't want to tell her because it was just a rumour. She couldn't figure out why everybody was being so nice to her! We had a secretary in those days, Miriam Davies, who later married Walter Gilbert. She'd been in the aviation business most of her life, so she'd been around and was hardened to accidents and other disasters. Well, Gilbert gets the word that Ballentine's gone down in flames and says, "The stupid bastard! The only guy with an airplane that's got an automatic fire extinguisher and he has to burn himself to a crisp!" Whereupon Miriam went to the can and was sick. What a tribute!

It was a great one-man business. When you left on a trip you were the vice-president of the company, you were the longshoreman, you were everything. You made your own decisions, you made your own mistakes, and you got your knuckles rapped, but nobody was very tough about it. Nobody expected you to be perfect, they just expected

you to try, and they stood up for their own people. When I went to work at CPA after those years at Canadian Airways—although I enjoyed the technical aspects of being an airline pilot and the nice equipment—an awful lot of the fun went out of it. Eventually it was one of the reasons I got out of the business. I was told by a guy, would I mind my own affairs and just fly airplanes? With Canadian Airways, or with any of the other companies, my affairs were the company's affairs and vice versa. If I saw a way to make money or a way to avoid losing money or a way to improve something, I was expected to speak up.

On the Vancouver–Victoria run in late '39 and '40 a great deal of our passenger load was government business, and because of the war there was a lot of travel to the capital. One of our most regular passengers was Attorney General Gordon Wismer, who was really quite a character. We got to know all the back ways into the Empress Hotel so we could deliver the body. One day I was down at the dock a little ahead of time and so was he, which was unusual. He was looking at the airplane, a twin engine DeHavilland Dragon Rapide that carried about seven passengers. The flight deck had room for one person, period. He said, "Where's the machine gun?"

It just rocked me on my heels. I said, "What machine gun?"

"You mean to say there's nothing up there? You're going over Esquimalt dry dock you know."

"Hell, there's hardly room up there for me."

"Well, of course you carry a gun yourself, a pistol or something?"

I didn't tell him I didn't need one, I told him I didn't have a licence to carry one. He said he'd see about that. In two days Walter Gilbert had orders to equip all coastal pilots with side arms. We thought this was great fun, very romantic. I was chief pilot at the time so I had to go around to all the shops in the Lower Mainland for all the pistols I could find. The Merchant Marine had got to most of the stores before I did but we managed to get everyone equipped. I carried mine in a shoulder holster so no one would know I had it on.

Actually it was a ridiculous requirement. The only time I had even the faintest possible use for it was when I had a drunken passenger who was by himself. He insisted on doing things I thought were dangerous, and because we were over water I couldn't stop him by getting out of my seat or landing. I was on the point of pulling out this damn pistol but before I did I thought, "If I pull it out there's only two things I can do with it. I can either shoot this guy, or I can put it back. In either case I'm in trouble." So I shot him with the fire extinguisher and radioed ahead for the police to meet us.

We used to have to guard all the planes during that part of the war. You couldn't leave a plane unguarded, so if you had to overnight someplace you either had to sleep in it or hire somebody to do it for you, which was a cursed nuisance. We also had to black out the plane going over Esquimalt, so we improvised curtains which we pulled about ten minutes out. The Department of Transport and the military required this because they felt a passenger could drop an incendiary device out the back door and we couldn't stop them.

Actually, carrying a pistol made sense if you were travelling in unorganized territory. We used to do it when we were working in the bush. Lots of times you didn't have room to carry a rifle, which was the sensible thing to do, so we would stick a .22 revolver in the map case. We could shoot a grouse or make a noise if we got lost. Making noise was the gun's most useful feature.

About a year later, in the summer, after I'd made about 1800 crossings on that run, Wismer says to me, "Where's your gun?" By this time it was hot and wearing a shoulder holster was a nuisance because it made me sweat under the straps. I told him it was in my map case. "Where's that?" It was in the dispatch office. He raised hell with me about that. A year later, I left and went on as captain on an airline route. I carried it with me in my map case for the rest of the war. Nobody bothered me about it again.

Going from visual flying to airline flying was a big jump. We had been doing the Vancouver–Victoria run on floats during the daylight hours so none of us had any training in instrument or night flying. TCA had hired enough US talent and training so that by the time they got going they had made a quantum leap in training and equipment – for ground staff as well as pilots. We went from bush flying to airline flying without the same advantages. We were doing it during wartime, for one thing, and we had no government money. In my view this created some serious problems.

The pressure was on Canadian Airways to run a night trip over to Patricia Bay airport so we could get mail back to meet a 6 a.m. eastbound TCA flight. I had the great privilege of being sent to Seattle to take a course in airline flying with Northwest Airlines. It was late '40 or early '41 and I was in Seattle for six weeks, but you don't take a course and come back a number one expert. All you've got is the basic 'how to do it' and then all of a sudden here you are flying airline. The aircraft was a funny little thing, a twin-engine Dragonfly. Fortunately the Department of Transport wouldn't let us carry passengers on it, just mail. That's what they felt about it and I agreed.

That was the worst job I ever had; it was the scariest because the airplane wasn't properly equipped to do the job and I was inexperienced. So were the mechanics who were looking after it. They were top notch engineers, but they hadn't had any training in servicing an IFR aircraft. It led to two or three quite hairy experiences for me. My own training was so minimal that I don't think I had many landings in a Lockheed 14 when I was dispatched with a full load for Whitehorse on instruments. As captain, mind you, I'd been flying for quite a while, and in the good old Canadian Airways pattern it was assumed that if you could fly one airplane you could fly any airplane. You could, to a degree. But on the bush side, the transition was so gradual that you hardly noticed the change. You'd get a better airplane this year and you could do something you couldn't do last year, but you were still using the same skills and physical judgment and so on.

When we started flying Vancouver–Whitehorse, the route was Vancouver, Prince George, Fort St. John, Fort Nelson, Watson Lake, and Whitehorse. Between Vancouver and Prince George they hadn't had time to build radio ranges, so we were unable to stay on a range all the way, and we had full authority to choose the route. I could go directly from Vancouver, past Squamish and Bridge River to Prince George, or I could go east to Hope and turn north there, or I could go all the way to Princeton. If I went to Princeton I had the east leg of the Vancouver radio range, the west leg of the Princeton range and the north leg of the Princeton range, then there was a long gap until I heard the south leg of the Prince George radio range. The choice was entirely mine. Once we lost a plane on a mountain, and I'm sure the root cause was that the captain was in a hurry and took a shortcut. It was a very bad night and I had chosen to come around the long way.

Things got tightened up. I'm not trying to shove blame on anybody: this was wartime and they didn't have time to do everything and they couldn't buy equipment. I know that Grant McConachie would have given us better equipment if he could have, but he couldn't buy it. We, CPA by this time, got two from TCA but we lost one of them that night just before Christmas in '42.

We often ran out of oxygen, and flying at 16–18,000 feet without oxygen can be a very tiring business. The military got it first. Fair enough; we weren't being shot at. I'd sooner go without oxygen than be shot at. The bottles would become exhausted because it was an eight-hour flight each way over I forget how many mountain ranges and our level was pretty high. We had rules about oxygen which we couldn't follow when we didn't have the stuff. Air crew were supposed to get it at 14,000. If you've got a shaky heart, at 14,000 you'll pass out. You just turn blue. It may not do any lasting harm but it'll put you to sleep. Drop down 1,000 feet and you wake up. Go up again, you go to sleep again. I was needing oxygen at lower and lower altitudes before I was through. I wouldn't realize it until I got home, but I was pooped.

I'll tell you something about the clothing we used to wear. We had a nice uniform, navy blue and patterned after the Royal Canadian Air Force. A captain of a domestic carrier had two braid rings on

D.H. Dragon Rapide. Two Gypsy Six engines, 200 h.p. each.

his sleeve, and the first officer had one. Each of us had a greatcoat, parka, ordinary peaked cap, white shirt, black tie and black shoes. So you leave Vancouver at forty degrees above in the winter and you end up in Whitehorse at forty degrees below. What do you wear? If you put on your Stanfields in Vancouver you'd be clammy before you got to Hope and cold from then on because you'd be wet. Coming back, if you'd put them on at the other end, you'd be steaming by the time you got to Prince George on the way home. I finally evolved my own system. I would wear a sweater that's easily taken off, but for the bottoms I wore flannelette pyjamas. I'd leave them hanging under my slacks and nobody knew I had them on. Somewhere around Prince George I would tuck them into my socks, take off my uniform shoes and put on a pair of felt slippers and my prairie overshoes. Actually this is the way the Inuit dress in winter; keep it loose until you need it, then tuck it in to trap the warm air. It was pretty comfortable. The uniform cap was only worn outside of the airplane. You couldn't wear it with headphones so we all had ski caps or something of that sort. By the time you put that on, and an oxygen mask, and wrapped a blanket around your shoulders, you were quite a sight.

When we lost that Lockheed 14 on the mountain we needed replacements. We got Boeing 247s, which were pretty antiquated. They were a nice kindly old plane to fly, but had no range, no oxygen, no nothing. The company was finally able to get Lockheed 18s and Lodestars, which were delightful planes. I loved them. In fact I loved the "14" until I got into the Lodestar. The Lodestar had lots of power, nice performance, and no vices that I ever discovered. The "14" was fine except it couldn't carry any ice.

To get ice off the propellers, you put the prop into fine pitch and start the engine screaming, and that throws chucks of ice onto the skin of the airplane. In fact, if you look at one of those planes you'll see it's double-skinned and has dents all along it from the ice being thrown off. On the wings there were "boots," as they called them, which were flat things like inner tubes, formed to fit the nose contour of the wings. They were operated by an air pump that caused them to expand and contract at different stages along the wing and cause the ice to be thrown off. But this was by no means a cure-all. The only cure-all for ice is to get the hell out of it. We learned that under certain circumstances it was something we could handle, under certain others, no way. If you get ice on the wing you wait a little while, then start to work and break it off. If it only breaks off on the nose, what's left? A nice sharp little ridge on which the next accumulation of ice forms, and pretty soon you've got a two-by-four lying across the top of your wing and it ceases to be a wing.

One flight with ice problems sticks in my memory. We were flying across the Rockies between Prince George and Fort St. John, which is the lowest part of the Rockies, 9,200 feet or so. We were at about 11,000, a nice comfortable margin, on instruments, nice smooth air, just like flying in milk. I had a good first officer with me, Ted West, a very competent young guy, and I was eating lunch. We got a smattering of ice. I sat there and looked at it for a minute, then

1940, Canadian Airways Rapide seaplane.

there was another little splatter, just sprinkles. I put my lunch down on the floor and as I did that it was just as if we were riding behind a truckload of stucco. In thirty seconds the airplane stalled going 145 miles per hour, fell off on one wing, and started down. There were four inches of ice out there—right then it had ceased to be an airplane! I grabbed hold of it, and the first officer's job was to keep the engines going with enough carburetor heat that it cost us power. We had everything up against the fire-wall, engines absolutely wide open, just screaming in fine pitch, and sinking and falling off on one wing or another. That was the most horrible sight I ever saw. It just didn't look like an airplane.

We flew through the Rockies below the peaks and never saw a bloody thing, but we came out the other side. Unfortunately for us, the ice all melted off before we got to Fort St. John, so nobody else got to see it. We flew back the same day about 2,000 feet higher and had no trouble at all. I promptly went to the Meteorological Office and told them what had happened. I wondered what I had done wrong but we couldn't find anything in the weather maps that would explain it. About a month later, Herbie Seagram, who was flying the same equipment across the Rockies for TCA, had the same thing happen to him over Crescent Valley. I got hold of Herbie to compare symptoms and it was a similar thing; all of a sudden you're a chunk of ice and down you go. We both decided that once a year God had to teach you who was boss.

I guess the last time I had hold of an airplane was when I flew a TCA Constellation from Edmonton to Vancouver, which I had absolutely no business flying! I was a passenger. I had worked for Pacific Western Airlines for five years. I'd gotten out of the business for ten years after the war and had gone back in for five years. We had a lot of business in Edmonton with the Dewline. I got on board a TCA flight one night and the stewardess came back and said, "Would Captain Ballentine please come up to the front end?" I went up there and it was a pilot I knew. He asked me if I wanted to fly it, saying, "Go on, get in." I thought he meant the first officer's seat but the first officer just sat there and the pilot got up. He said, "Go ahead, it's all yours, I'm going back to the cabin. Get in there." So I buckled myself in and gingerly took hold of it. An airplane is an airplane, but this one was really smooth. I said to the first officer, "You've got this on automatic pilot." He said he didn't, and I'm not sure to this day whether he did or not. I flew the thing all the way from Edmonton to the start of the turn into Vancouver. I don't know how nervous the first officer was but I enjoyed myself.

Every once in a while I think it would be nice to go back and fly, but what the hell for? I've got a sailboat and if it's a question of spending money I'd sooner spend it on a better boat. I don't want to fly around an airport and I can't afford to fly anyplace else. I think everybody hates to admit that they can't do what they used to do as a professional. I'm a little too old to fly airplanes.

I must say that I figure I was extremely fortunate to spend my time in this business during that period when the pioneers ahead of me had smoothed out a lot of the rough spots and made the airplane more reliable, but when the business was still very much an individual business. The beginnings of airline flying were fascinating as well, though I eventually got fed up with it. But that's another story.